National Wildlife Federation®

ATTRACTING BIRDS,
BUTTERFLIES, AND OTHER
BACKYARD WILDLIFE

Expanded Second Edition

National Wildlife Federation®

ATTRACTING BIRDS, BUTTERFLIES, AND OTHER BACKYARD WILDLIFE

Expanded Second Edition

David Mizejewski

CRE▲TIVE
HOMEOWNER®

Editor: Jeremy Hauck
Copy Editor: Amy Deputato
Designer: Wendy Reynolds
Indexer: Elizabeth Walker

ISBN 978-1-58011-818-7

Library of Congress Cataloging-in-Publication Data

Names: Mizejewski, David, author. | National Wildlife Federation, issuing
  body.
Title: National Wildlife Federation : attracting birds, butterflies and other
  backyard wildlife / David Mizejewski.
Other titles: Attracting birds, butterflies and other backyard wildlife
Description: Expanded second edition. | Mount Joy, PA : Creative Homeowner,
  [2019] | Includes bibliographical references and index.
Identifiers: LCCN 2019000507 | ISBN 9781580118187 (pbk. : alk. paper)
Subjects: LCSH: Gardening to attract wildlife. | Wildlife habitat
  improvement. | Wildlife attracting.
Classification: LCC QL59 .M59 2019 | DDC 333.95/4--dc23
LC record available at https://lccn.loc.gov/2019000507

We are always looking for talented authors. To submit an idea, please send a brief inquiry to acquisitions@foxchapelpublishing.com.

Printed in China

Current Printing (last digit)
10 9 8 7 6 5

Creative Homeowner®, *www.creativehomeowner.com*, is an imprint of New Design Originals Corporation and distributed exclusively in North America by Fox Chapel Publishing Company, Inc., 800-457-9112, 903 Square Street, Mount Joy, PA 17552, and in the United Kingdom by Grantham Book Service, Trent Road, Grantham, Lincolnshire, NG31 7XQ.

To Mom and Dad:

All those years of muddy clothes, poison ivy, and the zoo in my bedroom paid off.

Thanks for allowing me to pursue my passion for nature.

To Justin:

Thank you for building our own wild garden every step of the way with me.

Contents

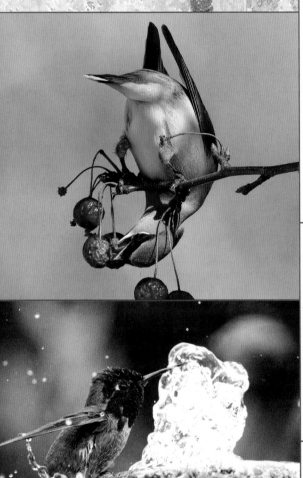

Preface to the Expanded Second Edition

Natural places and the wildlife species that inhabit them face ever-increasing pressure from human activity. Today, there are few places on Earth that have not been affected in some way by the way we've altered the planet. As a result, natural habitat is disappearing at an alarming rate and wildlife is declining.

Wildlife species and the natural areas they need to survive are important and should be protected and restored. Imagine life without the song of

birds and the chirring of crickets, the beauty of a windswept prairie, or the cool serenity of a green woodland. Imagine a child growing up without having the opportunity to watch a tadpole changing into a frog, to smell a wildflower, or to wade in a clear stream. Without wild areas, humanity, as well as wildlife, suffers.

It is easy to feel as if there is no hope for wildlife in our modern world of asphalt, smog, and traffic. But there is hope. You can choose to create a garden or landscape that helps restore habitat for local wildlife and the ecological balance. You can surround yourself with beautiful native plants that will attract an amazing array of birds, butterflies, and other backyard wildlife for you to enjoy, right outside your window, every day.

This book will teach you how to create a wildlife habitat garden, and how to have it recognized by the National Wildlife Federation® as an official Certified Wildlife Habitat® through the Garden for Wildlife™ program. In doing so, you will be doing your part to restore the ecology of the land on which you live and make sure wildlife thrives in a rapidly changing world.

Introduction

We need to reconnect our cities, towns, and neighborhoods back into the ecosystem they were once a part of.

Wildlife is declining at an unprecedented rate all around the planet. Unfortunately human activity is the most significant cause of this decline. Our land development and agricultural practices, pollution, alteration of rivers and wetlands, and climate change are increasingly changing America's landscape in ways that render it barren for wildlife or kill wildlife outright. As a result, today more than one-third of America's wildlife is at risk of extinction in the coming decades. While the situation sounds grim, you might be surprised to learn that you can help reverse this alarming decline for some species by creating your own wildlife habitat garden.

How can a garden save wildlife? You might think that wildlife conservation is something

that only happens in wilderness areas far from human development. Protecting and restoring wild areas continues to be critical to ensuring wildlife populations remain healthy, but the scope of human impact on the planet is so great that many wildlife species can't rely on wilderness areas alone. We need to reconnect our cities, towns, and neighborhoods back into the ecosystem they were once a part of by restoring the green infrastructure that supports local and migratory wildlife.

For example, thirty percent of North American birds are in steep decline, including some species that will use a well-planned wildlife habitat landscape in close proximity to people, such as bobolinks, wood thrushes, meadowlarks, Western tanagers, bobwhite quail, Florida scrub-jays, or rufous hummingbirds. Wildlife gardens can also help insects like the monarch butterfly, populations of which have plummeted in recent decades, or the once-common rusty-patched bumble bee, the first North American bee species to be listed as endangered. Wooded suburban yards have already helped the fisher, a member of the weasel family that was almost wiped out, to recover and

expand its range. Backyard nesting boxes have helped bluebird populations recover from the loss of natural nesting habitat, and in many areas birds such as purple martins and chimney swifts are dependent on structures provided by humans for nesting. Gopher tortoises and the dozens of other species that rely on their burrows for shelter only survive largely because people have protected or restored habitat for them on private property. Similarly, the New England cottontail is no longer being considered for listing as an endangered species due in big part to farmers and landowners who made the effort to restore their brushy, forest-edge habitat. Many species like these can thrive right alongside us, but only if we make sure they have enough habitat—and your own property or other garden space can be one piece of habitat that helps do just that.

While wildlife habitat gardens aren't going to save imperiled species such as polar bears or red wolves or sea turtles that require vast wilderness areas, they can make a big difference for many species of wildlife, helping to keep common species common and in some cases helping

CHECKLIST FOR ENJOYING WILDLIFE

☐ Field guide books and apps

☐ Binoculars

☐ Notebook and pencil

☐ Magnifying lens

☐ Camera

☐ Comfortable viewing places

species in trouble. Research has shown that wildlife habitat gardens support twice the wildlife and a greater diversity of species compared to a conventional landscape of lawn and other non-native plants. They also give us a daily connection to nature that's sorely lacking from most of our lives, yet important, not only for our own happiness but also to inspire us to support broader wildlife conservation efforts.

Creating a wildlife habitat garden is more than just planting a pretty landscape. In any given region, the plants, animals, and other living organisms have interacted with one other and the environment around them for millions of years, forming interacting communities called an ecosystem. Ecosystems are healthy when they are diverse, self-sustaining, and balanced, with no one species dominating all the rest. This is true in wild ecosystems as well as in those in our cities, towns, and even our own yards and gardens. If you understand this principle and apply it to your garden and landscape, you'll create a beautiful mini-ecosystem that supports birds, butterflies, and a wide variety of other wildlife species.

Here's how it works. Plants are the foundation of wildlife habitat. Without healthy plant communities to provide habitat, wildlife disappears. By preserving or planting the native plants that naturally grow in the area and that wildlife need to survive, you can restore habitat and invite the wildlife back to the land it once occupied. The act of planting for a purpose is the very definition of gardening. By planting native plants to restore wildlife habitat, you become a wildlife habitat gardener.

The National Wildlife Federation's Garden for Wildlife program has been helping people do just this for over four decades. Millions of people have already restored natural habitat in their yards and other garden spaces throughout their communities. Hundreds of thousands have earned Certified Wildlife Habitat recognition for those wildlife habitat gardens. Today, these people host the wildlife that would otherwise be banished from our cities, towns, and neighborhoods. By applying what you learn in this book, you can join the National Wildlife Federation's growing Garden for Wildlife movement.

CHAPTER ONE

Getting Started

Gardens by their very nature are works of art designed to welcome people. Your challenge is to create a garden that meets the needs of wildlife by restoring natural habitat but still draws you and your family, neighbors, and friends into it. Look to natural wilderness for design inspiration. Keep this guiding principle in mind when you design your wildlife habitat garden.

Monarch butterflies sip nectar from purple coneflowers. Monarchs have declined significantly in recent decades. Planting native plants that offer nectar can help them recover.

Assessing Your Property

Begin by assessing your current landscape to determine what you already have and its condition. Use the following lists as guides. You'll find it helpful to actually write down the answers to these questions.

☐ What plant species do you already have?

_____

☐ What plant communities are represented?

_____

☐ Which of your plants are native? Non-native? Invasive?

_____

☐ Are any plantings overgrown or out of place?

_____

☐ What percentage of the property is lawn?

_____

☐ How much lawn do you and your family actually use?

_____

☐ What types of soils occur on your property?

_____

☐ What is the direction of the prominent wind?

_____

☐ What is the sun exposure for each part of the property?

_____

☐ What microclimates exist on the property?

_____

☐ What is the topography of the property? Which areas are low and retain water, and which areas are higher and drier?

_____

☐ What is the location of any underground power lines?

_____

☐ Are there any entry points where wildlife might gain access to your house that need repair?

_____

☐ How will your neighbors take to a naturalistic landscape?

_____

Create a wish list for the plants and other features you want in your wildlife habitat garden. Use the following ideas as a guideline:

☐ What percentage of the property do you want to devote to wildlife gardening and how much needs to be kept mowed or open for human use?

_____

_____

☐ What kinds of wildlife do you want to attract?

_____

_____

☐ What is your budget?

_____

_____

☐ What colors would you like to see in the garden?

_____

_____

☐ What hardscape features, such as patios, retaining walls, gazebos, or other structures, would you like?

_____

_____

☐ Do you need play areas for children?

_____

_____

☐ Are there any special viewing points that you'd like to preserve or create?

_____

_____

☐ What are the top priorities for this season? Next season?

_____

_____

Identify Your Plants

Identify the plants that currently grow in your yard and neighborhood. Take photos and use online gardening sites, garden plant apps, or gardening books, or bring your photos to your local nursery for identification help. You'll be surprised to find that many of the plants used in landscapes are not native. Instead they come from other parts of the world and were chosen because of their beauty or functionality in the landscape. Ability to grow in poor soils, to withstand air pollution, to provide ornamental blooms and foliage, and to resist disease are plant characteristics that typically outweigh a plant's value to wildlife when people choose plants for their gardens. Many common species that you've seen your entire life are really non-natives that have been introduced in just the last century. The fact that you are used to seeing them and may mistake them for natural parts of the ecosystem does not change their negative impact on native plant and wildlife species.

Restoring Native Plants

Plants are the tools you will use to create your wildlife habitat garden and connect your property back into the local ecosystem. Native wildlife species have evolved to depend on the plants that are also native to their ecosystem.

Native plants are adapted to the range of seasonal conditions in their region. This means that they have evolved to thrive in the natural soils, climate, weather, rainfall, and sun exposure of their native region. Wildlife species evolved to take advantage of the resources provided by these native plants. Without them, wildlife populations decline. As a result, only native plants provide the entire range of habitat benefits needed by native wildlife.

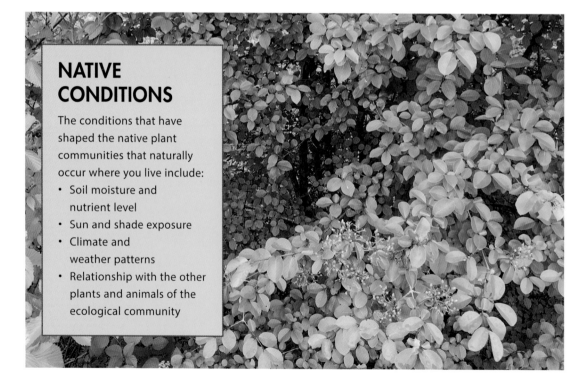

NATIVE CONDITIONS

The conditions that have shaped the native plant communities that naturally occur where you live include:

- Soil moisture and nutrient level
- Sun and shade exposure
- Climate and weather patterns
- Relationship with the other plants and animals of the ecological community

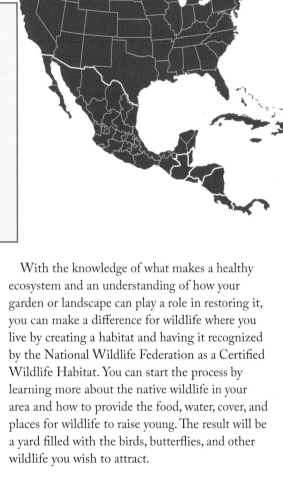

NATIVE TO NORTH AMERICA

This book is for gardeners and wildlife enthusiasts in North America. When the term "native species" is used it refers to species native to North America. Few species have a native distribution over the entire continent, so consult with your state's native plant society, natural resources agency, or local naturalists to determine which species naturally grow locally where you live. Visit the National Wildlife Federation's Garden for Wildlife website for more native plant resources at *www.nwf.org/garden*.

THE PROBLEMS WITH NON-NATIVE PLANTS

- Non-natives can become invasive and degrade naturally diverse ecosystems.
- Non-natives can introduce and harbor diseases that afflict native species.
- Non-native plants do not support native wildlife species.
- Some non-natives require costly maintenance and wasteful watering and chemicals.
- *See page 136 for more info on non-native plants.*

Native plants are great choices for your landscape. When planted in their natural conditions, they require almost no maintenance once they are established. While they are establishing themselves, native plants might need supplemental watering. It can take as little as a few weeks for natives to become established and rarely takes longer than one growing season. Planting natives can mean a significant reduction in the amount of pesticides and fertilizers released into the environment and can eliminate the need for supplemental watering.

With the knowledge of what makes a healthy ecosystem and an understanding of how your garden or landscape can play a role in restoring it, you can make a difference for wildlife where you live by creating a habitat and having it recognized by the National Wildlife Federation as a Certified Wildlife Habitat. You can start the process by learning more about the native wildlife in your area and how to provide the food, water, cover, and places for wildlife to raise young. The result will be a yard filled with the birds, butterflies, and other wildlife you wish to attract.

Purchasing Native Plants

Your wildlife habitat garden should have as many native plant species as possible. Native plants are the foundation of habitat in the wild and should be in your wildlife habitat garden, too.

Some native species have been garden center staples for years. For example, native dogwoods (*Cornus* spp.), coneflower (*Echinacea* spp.), black-eyed Susans (*Rudbeckia* spp.), and blueberries (*Vaccinium* spp.) have long been cultivated as ornamentals. Even so, finding a great variety of natives at your local garden center can still sometimes be challenging. The horticulture and landscaping industries are just beginning to recognize the ecological and economic value of working with native plants. Some companies label native species to make it easier for native plant enthusiasts to find the appropriate plants.

FINDING NATIVE PLANTS

- Contact your local native plant society to learn what plants are native to your region and which are invasives or other problematic non-natives.
- Learn how to propagate plants from seeds and cuttings and grow your own native plants.
- Participate in plant swaps with other native plant growers.
- Organize a plant rescue at a construction site.
- Let your local nursery know you will purchase native plants for wildlife if they are available and clearly marked as native.
- Patronize nurseries that carry native plants.
- Visit *www.nwf.org/garden* for more native plant resources.

HOW NATIVE PLANTS ARE SOLD

Native plants are sold in a variety of different ways:

Seed. Herbaceous (see Glossary, page 161) grasses and wildflowers are generally sold as seed, although some woody (see Glossary, page 165) species are also available as seed. Work with a nursery that specializes in native seeds for your area. Don't purchase seed mixes in a can as they often contain invasive non-native species.

Plug. Plugs are seedlings of both herbaceous and woody plants that are usually one or two years old. Plugs are usually grown in narrow containers and sold with a small, dense root-ball. Because plugs are small and relatively inexpensive, they are also a good choice for covering large areas.

Plug

Whip. Whips are the cut branches of willow, poplar, and other woody species that will root from branch cuttings. Whips can be planted upright directly into the soil or placed horizontally in a shallow trench and then covered with soil. Whips are often used on slopes to control erosion of wetland areas. They are also relatively inexpensive.

Bare-root

Bare-root. Both herbaceous and woody plant species are sold bare-root, which means all soil or other growing medium has been washed away from the root-ball. Bare-root plants are typically sold via mail order while dormant, and they are relatively inexpensive.

Containerized or potted. Both herbaceous and woody plants are sold in containers or pots, typically by retailers. Like the balled-and-burlapped stock, containerized plants are usually too heavy for shipping and require significant care in the retail nursery setting, and are therefore more expensive.

Containerized

Balled-and-burlapped. Large woody plants are typically sold in a retail nursery setting with their root-balls, complete with soil, wrapped in burlap. The plant's weight, size, and necessary care by a retail nursery (its overhead costs) increase the cost of balled-and-burlapped (often abbreviated as "B-and-B") stock and make mail-order sales prohibitively difficult and expensive. But B-and-B stock will have an instant effect on the landscape.

Balled-and-burlapped

Many native plant species are highly ornamental and available for sale at your local nursery. Some are long-time garden staples, like this flowering dogwood.

Many nurseries that sell native plants often offer only specially bred or cloned hybrids or cultivars that have been chosen for their landscape value or appearance. A variety is a particular type of a species. Varieties occur naturally or are created by people through selective breeding. A cultivar (short for cultivated variety) is a variety that has been created by people via breeding or cloning. Unfortunately, selective breeding for ornamental qualities alone often affects the qualities that made the original plant species beneficial to wildlife, and cloning can result in a loss of the genetic diversity that occurs naturally in the wild.

For example, cultivars with blooms that are larger or a different shape often prevent pollinators from accessing the nectar and pollen within. Insects such as bees can see ultraviolet light not visible to the human eye. Many flowers have ultraviolet coloration to attract bees that

we cannot see. We can easily inadvertently breed out such features and render a cultivar useless to wildlife without even knowing it.

You can identify which plants are cultivars by looking at the names on their plant tags or plant descriptions. Every plant has a common name and a scientific name. The common name of a plant is written first, followed by the italicized scientific name in parentheses. An example of this is river birch (*Betula nigra*). Cultivars are given special names by their breeders or cloners. These special names are listed in quotation marks on the plant tag after the common and scientific names. A popular cultivar of river birch is 'Heritage'. The plant tag for this cultivar would read River Birch (*Betula nigra* 'Heritage'). Hybrids are indicated by an "x" in the scientific name. An example of this is the hybrid cultivar of two shrubs, fragrant sage (*Salvia clevelandii*) and purple sage (*Salvia leucophylla*), both western natives. The hybrid name is gray musk sage (*Salvia clevelandii* x *leucophylla* 'Pozo Blue').

Reading plant tags will give you important information that will help you make your plant selections. Cultivars and hybrids of natives aren't necessarily bad choices for wildlife, and often they are the only options available through retail garden centers. Think of cultivars and hybrids as domesticated versions of wild plants. Releasing packs of domestic dogs into the wild isn't the same thing as restoring gray wolf populations, even though all dogs are descended from wolves. Sticking to the original native plant species or cultivars that are as close to the wild native in appearance as possible is the best plan if you're working to restore a functioning bit of the ecosystem. They are certainly better choices than lawn or non-native plants when it comes to wildlife habitat in a landscape or garden setting.

Native Plant Societies and Nurseries

There are many ways to learn which plant species are native. Field guides are a good place to start; just keep in mind they sometimes include all the species that you might commonly see in a particular region, both native and non-native. A regional native plant guide is better and an internet search will deliver many results. Contacting your local or state native plant societies can provide the most reliable information. They are dedicated to preserving and restoring the natural floral heritage of their region. Most have excellent native plant lists that can be obtained free of charge. Many hold annual native plant sales, and members themselves are often a wonderful source of native plants grown in their own gardens.

Most native plant societies can provide you with a list of native plant nurseries in your area.

Replace lawn with beds of blooming native plants. They're beautiful and will attract equally beautiful wildlife for you to enjoy.

Every region has its own diverse native plant options. Here a desert cottontail feasts on prickly pear cactus fruit in an Arizona wildlife habitat garden.

Today, most garden centers carry some natives, and many even label them as such. There are even some nurseries that specialize in native plants. If you don't have a nursery that carries native plants nearby, you can order them online or via catalogs. Plants shipped to you are often sent bare-root, which means that all the soil has been washed away from their roots. Not only does this make them lighter for shipping, it often reduces the cost of the plants because it's cheaper for the nursery to grow them in beds instead of containers.

Participating in Plant Rescues

Organized "plant rescues" provide another great way to get plants that are native to your area.

Native plant societies or other conservation organizations often conduct the rescues, which take place in areas slated for development with the permission of the property owner. Not only does this save locally native plants from certain destruction, it is a free source of plant material for your garden.

Never collect plants from the wild unless you are participating in an authorized plant rescue. Many species have been pushed to the brink of extinction as a result of overenthusiastic plant collectors digging from the wild. Don't patronize nurseries that dig their plants from the wild. Ask to make sure that the plants for sale were both propagated and grown in the nursery. Be specific. A plant that was dug in the wild and then grown in a pot for a year might be labeled as "nursery grown."

Garden Design Approaches

Once you've assessed your property, gained a sense of the site-specific conditions, and done some research on native plant resources for your area, you're ready to start planting. The design of the garden or landscape is just as important as the plants you select. Conventional planting approaches offer limited habitat for wildlife. Here are some alternative planting approaches that will help you design your habitat.

The Wait-and-See Approach

Allowing the plants you already have to grow freely and spread is one way of creating habitat. Rigidly pruned plants, when left to grow in a more natural, less contained way, will provide more cover for wildlife. Left to grow, a lawn or manicured garden will follow the natural process of succession, and other species will begin to colonize.

There are some downsides to this approach. Keep in mind that it may be difficult for the seeds of native plants to make their way into your garden naturally by wind or wildlife, especially if you live somewhere that doesn't have wild areas nearby to serve as seed sources. The seeds that do show up may be from invasive non-native species. The same wild look that will be attractive to wildlife may be decidedly unattractive to your neighbors. Be sure to talk with your neighbors and explain why you're creating a naturalistic landscape.

Native plants provide birds such as this goldfinch with natural sources of food and nesting material.

The Bull's-Eye Approach

Another planting option for those who cannot have a completely wild landscape is the "bull's-eye" approach. Think of your house—the human habitat—as the center of a bull's eye surrounded by concentric planting rings. You can begin with the first planting ring, the one surrounding the house, by creating planting beds around the foundation. If you are going to feature ornamental non-native species (noninvasive, of course) or would like to showcase a neat and formal planting design, this is the best place to do it.

The second ring is the place for lawn. You'll want to keep in mind your specific use of lawn and determine how much you actually need and use, but surrounding your foundation planting with a bit of lawn will also help give your property an orderly appearance.

Beyond the foundation and lawn is where the real fun begins. Maybe you'll let the lawn transition into a meadow or prairie patch. Or you can let the lawn blend into a rain garden or wetland area, perhaps with a pond, where

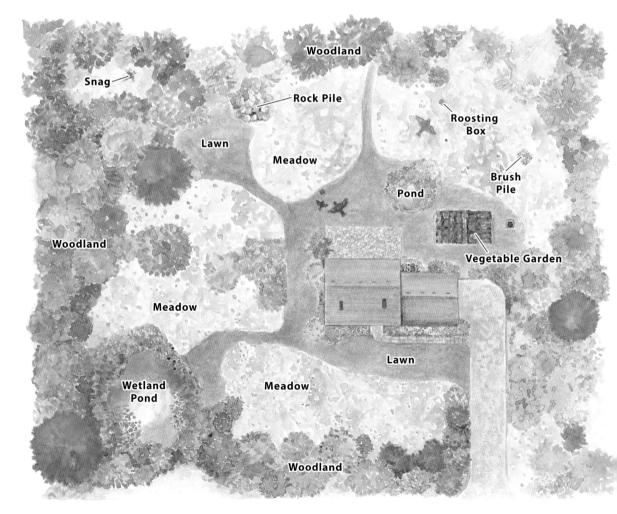

When designing your wildlife habitat garden, look to Mother Nature for inspiration. Use native species, plant densely, and plan for year-round interest—both for you and wildlife.

the yard naturally dips toward the back of the property. Behind the grassland or wetland area, you may want to plant a shrub row or a bramble patch, or allow the woody scrub to mix with the herbaceous grasses and wildflowers. If you live in an area where forests naturally occur, you can create and nurture a corner woodland pocket at the back, or even around the entire perimeter, of the property.

By using the bull's-eye approach, you can also take advantage of the edge effect. The edge effect refers to the greater diversity of wildlife that normally occurs where two different plant communities or ecosystems meet. For example, a meadow or prairie garden that abuts a wooded area might support both grasslands birds and woodland birds, along with generalist species that can survive in either habitat.

The Remove-and-Replace Approach

Remove plants that are invasive or have little value to wildlife, and replace them with native species that are appropriate for your site. In this way, you can slowly change a relatively sterile, conventional landscape into a more productive, native-based one. The benefit of this approach is that you can make as many or as few changes as your time and budget will allow within a given season. Another benefit is that this habitat style can mimic popular garden designs. For example, if your garden is planted in a formal style or your plantings follow a particular color scheme, you can keep the design and preserve the look you enjoy by replacing problematic non-native plants with similarly sized and colored native ones that are suited to the site.

Design your habitat garden to be attractive to local wildlife, but also include focal points, like this natural water garden, that are pleasing for people to look at, too.

The Holistic Approach

The ultimate goal of creating a naturalistic, wildlife-friendly landscape is to restore a small piece of the natural ecosystem. The best way to accomplish this is to become an expert on the land upon which you live, learn its healthy and not-so-healthy aspects, and begin to coax it back into natural productivity and diversity. This holistic approach is very in-depth, but it will be the most rewarding for you and wildlife. Each of the previously described planting approaches can be incorporated into the holistic design method.

You can begin this process by doing some research and learning the natural history of the greater region that includes your property. Look to the natural areas around you for inspiration and to begin to learn what kind of native plant communities, in all stages of succession, occur in your area. Ask questions. What species of plants and animals existed where you now live a hundred years ago? Do they still occur? If those species are no longer present in the landscape, why did they disappear? You'll want to learn the human history of the land as well, going all the way back to its first human inhabitants. How did your predecessors throughout history make a living from and affect the land? Which historical practices were sustainable, and which ones have led to environmental degradation? How many times has the natural vegetation been removed and regenerated? What non-native plants and animals have been introduced and become invasive? What are the natural soil types of the area, and in what condition is the soil now?

You can answer many of these questions by making a trip to your town hall. The planning and zoning commission should have historical information and sometimes even aerial photographs of your property and the surrounding land. The city or town's taxation department will have historical plat maps of your property and those that are adjacent to it. The local library, county extension service, native plant society, and historical society will all be helpful resources in your research as well.

Each question you ask will reveal clues about what you will need to do to restore habitat and the overall health of the land. You don't have to spend endless hours doing this research, but the information that you find will make you intimately familiar with the land upon which you currently live and will be invaluable to you as you plan your landscape.

As you explore the possibilities, consider the size of the space that you want to devote to habitat and the kinds of animals for which you'd like to provide. Your goal should be to provide a balanced ecosystem for a great variety of native wildlife. That doesn't mean you must provide for every species. Some wildlife cannot or should not live in close proximity to humans. Attracting large or predatory wildlife species, if they live in your area, can be dangerous for both people and wildlife. Fight to protect wilderness areas for those species, while doing what you can in your yard for species that can safely coexist with people.

Once you know the areas that need to be enhanced, you can begin selecting native plant species suited to the site. Most likely you won't be able to accomplish everything at once. It's all right to start small and take on one project at a time. You should enjoy habitat gardening year after year, making changes and improvements as you learn. By taking a holistic approach to habitat restoration, you can make even the smallest piece of land into a productive mini ecosystem teeming with wildlife.

Filling your garden with blooming plants will attract butterflies, bees, and other pollinators. Native plants are best, but even tried-and-true annual zinnias provide a nectar source.

Special Considerations for Urban Habitats

Whether the location is a balcony, a rooftop, an alley, or even a small city yard, urban habitat gardeners face a unique set of challenges. Many people believe that few species of wildlife will visit urban habitat gardens. On the contrary, providing

habitat in urban areas can be even more important than providing it in suburban areas, where some resources for wildlife still exist. Urban wildlife species face the same daily challenges that their human counterparts face: lack of plants, little open space, trash, noise, and pollution. While it's true that not all wildlife species can tolerate urban conditions, a green urban oasis will be used and relished by a surprising array of city-living wildlife species.

The species that will be able to access your urban habitat area might be somewhat different from the species that will visit suburban and rural areas. Most large wildlife species won't make their way into urban centers. Neither will those species that have very specific habitat requirements, like deep forests or open grassland—although you may be surprised at the adaptability of many species. Birds will definitely show up in a city habitat, and not just pigeons. A wide array of local and migratory songbirds and even raptors will visit urban gardens if the habitat is there. They may even nest and lay eggs as well. Landscape features that could attract or harbor rats, including bird feeders and brush piles, are usually not good options in urban habitat gardens.

The next challenge faced by urban wildlife gardeners is the limited amount of available space for gardening. Another is poor-quality or severely compacted urban soil, or even a complete lack of unpaved surfaces in which to plant. Additionally, many people living in urban areas rent their homes or apartments and do not want to invest in plants that they can't take with them if they move. Container gardening, raised beds, and window boxes are great solutions to these challenges. Native wildflowers, grasses, shrubs, and even small trees can thrive in pots if they are well watered and periodically fertilized.

Coreopsis

Oregano

Phlox

Sunflower

BEST CONTAINER PLANTS

These common garden plants, some of which are North American natives, do well in containers and provide some element of habitat. Some provide hummingbirds and insects such as butterflies with nectar, while others are also host plants for butterfly caterpillars or produce seeds that will be eaten by birds.

- Clematis (*Clematis* spp.)
- **Coreopsis (*Coreopsis* spp.)**
- Dianthus (*Dianthus* spp.)
- Flowering tobacco (*Nicotiana* spp.)
- Lantana (*Lantana* spp.)
- Lavender (*Lavandula* spp.)
- Marigold (*Tagetes* spp.)
- Mint (*Mentha* spp.)
- Morning glory (*Ipomoea* spp.)
- Nasturtium (*Tropaeolum* spp.)
- **Oregano (*Origanum* spp.)**
- Parsley (*Petroselinum* spp.)
- **Phlox (*Phlox* spp.)**
- Rosemary (*Rosmarinus* spp.)
- Salvia (*Salvia* spp.)
- Sedum (*Sedum* spp.)
- **Sunflower (*Helianthus* spp.)**
- Verbena (*Verbena* spp.)
- Yarrow (*Achillea* spp.)
- Zinnia (*Zinnia* spp.)

Special Considerations for Rural Habitats

Rural properties offer opportunities for providing wildlife habitat that are different from urban or suburban properties. Rural areas often already have higher wildlife populations and a greater diversity of species than do other areas with denser human populations. For this reason, people living in rural areas may not see the need to create and restore places for wildlife. The reality is that even rural areas have been affected by human encroachment, and in many places habitat has been degraded by new roads, new development, invasive non-native species, livestock and other domestic animals, waste runoff from factory farms, and heavy use of chemical pesticides and fertilizers. Large tracts of land in rural areas often provide critical habitat for larger and potentially dangerous wildlife species. Learn which species may live on or use your property.

GET INSPIRATION

Once known for exotic plants from around the world, botanical gardens are increasingly including native plant species in their collections and public gardens. Likewise, many zoos and aquariums have incorporated native plants and installed demonstration wildlife habitat garden areas as a way to inspire visitors to take their conservation messages home and make a difference for wildlife locally.

Many of these public garden spaces participate in the Garden for Wildlife program. The Denver Zoo, the U.S. Botanic Garden in Washington DC, both Disney's Epcot and Animal Kingdom theme parks in Orlando, and even Camden Yards (the Baltimore Orioles baseball stadium) are just a few of the many public spaces that have been recognized as Certified Wildlife Habitat by the National Wildlife Federation.

A visit to one of these gardens can give you ideas and inspiration as you plan your own wildlife habitat garden.

Wildlife habitat gardens are a beautiful part of the local ecosystem that support wonderful wildlife from birds to butterflies, unlike conventional landscapes made up of barren lawns and non-native plants that support nothing. This example can be found at the Denver Botanic Gardens.

It is important to learn how to provide for these species in a way that is safest for people as well as the wildlife. Species like black bears will be attracted to pet and livestock food that is stored outside. Bird feeders may not be a good idea in areas with healthy bear populations. Living near wildlife like deer may also mean living near deer predators like mountain lions. Large hoofed animals like moose and elk can also be dangerous. In Florida and the coastal south, alligators might be present on properties that include wetlands.

Never try to touch or pet any wildlife species, no matter how cute or tame it looks. By keeping the unique circumstances—and opportunities—of owning and managing a large tract of rural land in mind, you will be able to safely view and appreciate these larger creatures.

Critter-Proof Your Home

While you love wildlife and want to make sure it has a habitat in which to live, you don't want it moving into your home. Critter-proofing your house is always a good idea, and even more so when you are creating a habitat garden to attract wildlife.

Inspect your roofline annually and make sure there are no access points for wildlife such as bats, wasps, squirrels, or raccoons. Similarly, inspect your foundation or crawlspace for entry points. Don't forget your porch or shed, which will be happily used as a hiding or denning place for groundhogs, snakes, foxes, or skunks. If you keep your windows open, be sure they are covered in screens. Same for doors.

If you do find a wild animal in your home, never try to handle it. Instead, try to restrict it to one room and leave an exterior door or window open in that room. Wildlife will almost always find their own way out. You can also contact a professional wildlife removal company or a licensed wildlife rehabilitator to assist you. Prevention is worth a pound of cure in these instances.

DO YOU OWN A NEWLY BUILT HOUSE?

BUILDING WITHIN THE ENVELOPE

If you are building a new house on an undeveloped lot, survey the plant communities that already exist there. If one portion of the property has a healthy plant community, consider preserving that area and locate the house, if possible, in an area covered in invasive non-natives or less-established plants. Save the trees that provide the best value to local wildlife. Remember that fallen or dying trees provide a lot of wildlife habitat.

Once you've identified the plants that you want to save, work with the contractor to protect the vegetation from damage during construction. Mark these areas with white construction ribbon (available at most hardware stores or home centers).

Protect the root zones of individual trees by blocking off the area to prevent heavy equipment from compacting the roots. To determine how far the underground roots extend, multiply the diameter of the tree trunk by 1.2.

The end result should be an "envelope" of vegetation around the site of the new house that is clearly marked off and safe from damage by machinery. The contractor and his machinery will then operate entirely within this envelope during construction, and you will have a beautiful, established habitat when you move into your new house.

STARTING FROM SCRATCH

If you have recently moved into a newly built house, you may find yourself the proud owner of a piece of land that has been scraped clean of every bit of vegetation as well as the original topsoil. You will be starting with a blank canvas on which you can build your wildlife garden. The entire property may be seeded with lawn grass. Begin defining beds and other habitat features as soon as possible, before your lawn is established.

Resist the urge to buy prepackaged "wildflower" seed mixes, because they may contain invasive non-native species.

HABITAT FOR KIDS

Children, too, will benefit from your habitat. Kids love secret spots in the garden where they can hide, think, get away from adults for a time, and connect with the natural world at their own pace. In today's modern society, children need outdoor experiences to introduce them to the natural wonders of the plants and animals that share their space. Allow the children in your life to assist in the creation of your habitat, and begin teaching them stewardship at an early age.

Your Place in Your Wildlife Habitat Garden

Providing habitat for wildlife involves more than the science of ecology and wildlife populations. It is also about connecting with nature where you live in a personal way. If you have kids, it can also be about fostering the next generation of conservation stewards, and spreading your knowledge to help others create habitat.

When creating a wildlife habitat garden, remember to make a place for people as well. As you define your planting areas, look critically at your true usage of the landscape. Few people actually use their entire lawn area, for example. Perhaps you'd like an area of lawn for your annual family reunion or church picnic, or a play area for your children or grandchildren. Lawns can add definition to the more wild areas of your property, and they can provide viewpoints from your house or patio. Beyond those true uses of lawn, the rest of your property can be planted in a more natural fashion.

This doesn't mean that you won't ever visit the wilder parts of your property. On the contrary, you should be sure to plan space for people in your habitat areas, too. A wooden bench or mossy green spot near a small pond or under a shade tree can be your own private haven to escape, unwind, relax, and observe the wonderful wildlife that live in your habitat.

You can create paths through natural areas by simply mowing a swath through a planted area or along its perimeter. Follow the curves of your garden beds or look to the natural topography of the land to give you an idea of where your path should be. You can use mulch or gravel to create paths as well.

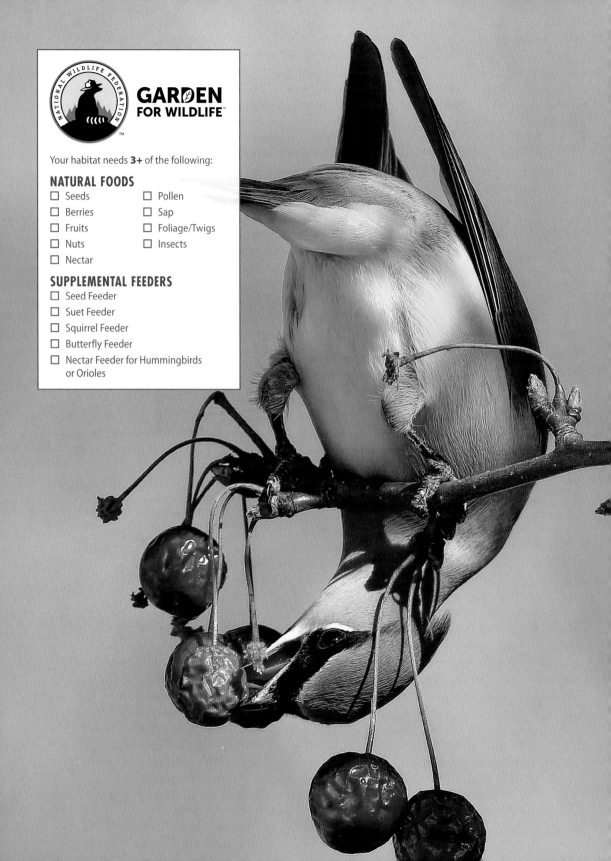

GARDEN
FOR WILDLIFE™

Your habitat needs **3+** of the following:

NATURAL FOODS

☐ Seeds   ☐ Pollen

☐ Berries   ☐ Sap

☐ Fruits   ☐ Foliage/Twigs

☐ Nuts   ☐ Insects

☐ Nectar

SUPPLEMENTAL FEEDERS

☐ Seed Feeder

☐ Suet Feeder

☐ Squirrel Feeder

☐ Butterfly Feeder

☐ Nectar Feeder for Hummingbirds
  or Orioles

CHAPTER TWO

Food

Food is the first habitat component to provide in your wildlife habitat garden. The most important way to offer food is through native plants. Natives offer natural food sources such as seeds, berries, nuts, foliage, pollen, and nectar. The insects supported by native plants also become food for birds and other wildlife.

Plants provide natural food sources for birds, such as this cedar waxwing dining on a berry. Restoring native plant communities is the best way to feed wildlife.

The food web is a concept used to describe the process of how nutrients travel through the ecosystem and sustain wildlife. Plants capture energy from the sun and absorb water and minerals from the soil to produce nutrients for themselves in the form of carbohydrates. For this reason, plants are called "producers" and form the foundation of the food web.

"Consumers" are organisms that cannot create their own nutrients, but instead rely on producers and other consumers as food sources. All animals, including birds, mammals, fish, reptiles, amphibians, and insects and other invertebrates, are consumers. Some consumers rely solely on plants as their food source, while other consumers rely on other animals for food. Some species consume both plants and animals.

Threads in the Food Web

Every wildlife species provides a thread in the food web. As consumers eat plants and other animals, they transfer the energy from the sun and the nutrients produced by plants further along the food web. Eventually, these nutrients end up in the body of an animal that has no natural predators. When these top consumers eventually die, organisms called decomposers recycle the nutrients found in the bodies of consumers back into the raw materials needed by producers to make food. Decomposers also help break down dead plant material. When these nutrients are recycled back into the soil, they are once again available for plants and the cycle begins anew.

The landscape you create can be a mini-ecosystem with a functioning food web. Providing food for wildlife is more than just putting out feeders. Your task is to build a food web and restore balance to the ecosystem. That may sound complicated, but it's easier than you think. As a wildlife habitat gardener, you are simply selecting which producers—native plants—will be part of your landscape. The producers provide for and attract the consumers, and the rest of the food web falls into place. You can affect the types and numbers of wildlife species that you attract by your plant choices and garden design.

Native predators are an important part of any ecosystem, including your garden. Here a long-tailed weasel helps keep the rodent population in check.

The Role of Predators

Predators play an important role in the food web. They help keep the ecosystem balanced by keeping the populations of prey species in check. When predators are present, ecosystems are diverse, resilient, and healthier—including the ecosystem in your own garden. While you shouldn't try to attract large predators such as bears, mountain lions, or alligators to your yard, there's a surprising diversity of smaller predators that will help your wildlife habitat garden thrive.

Spiders. Some spiders spin webs to catch a meal while others stalk their prey. They are important predators of insects, including most biting and plant-eating varieties.

Beetles. There are 25,000 beetle species in North America and many of them, including ladybugs, tiger beetles, soldier beetles, ground

Spiders (above) and predatory beetles such as ladybugs consume garden pests.

Salamanders such as this red eft—the juvenile form of the red-spotted newt—are voracious predators of insects and other invertebrates.

All owl species are predators. Burrowing owls eat insects, reptiles, and rodents.

Damselflies pluck flying insects right out of the air.

beetles, and even fireflies, are predators that help keep pests in check.

Salamanders. All salamanders are carnivorous, eating insects, worms, slugs, and other invertebrates. The aquatic hatchlings of these amphibians are predators of mosquito larvae.

Owls. Owls are incredibly silent in flight, aided by sound-suppressing fuzz that covers their flight feathers. They are able to rapidly locate and kill small mammals, birds, and insects in complete silence.

Other backyard predators that are commonly found throughout North America include dragonflies, opossums, bats, mantids, foxes, snakes, and even songbirds, most species of which prey on insects.

WILDLIFE PROFILE:
VIRGINIA OPOSSUM

The Virginia opossum is a wonderful creature found over much of North America that should be welcome in your wildlife habitat garden.

Though often misidentified as "big rats," opossums are not rodents at all despite a superficial resemblance. They are North America's only marsupial, mammals that give birth to tiny, blind young that crawl into their mother's pouch where they nurse and complete development. They often ride on their mother's back once they've become too big for the pouch.

Opossums are omnivores, eating a variety of foods from fruits to insects to rodents. They also happily feed on carrion. This generalist diet has allowed opossums to survive hundreds of millions of years. Opossums also feed on snakes, including venomous ones, and have a natural resistance to venom.

Opossums are also fastidious groomers. As a result, they are one of the best natural controls on tick populations. In one season, an opossum can consume 5,000 ticks that it has groomed off itself. That's 5,000 fewer ticks to bite you or your pets.

As with all mammals, don't feed opossums. You can support them by preserving mature trees on your property and planting a lot of native plants and building a natural food web.

KEEP CATS OUT OF THE NATURAL FOOD WEB

If you have a pet cat, it's important to keep it safely indoors so it doesn't kill the wildlife you attract to your habitat garden. Domesticated cats are not native to North America and their predation is taking an enormous toll on native wildlife.

The U.S. Fish and Wildlife Service and the Smithsonian Institution have conservatively estimated that free-ranging domesticated cats kill up to 4 billion birds and over 22 billion mammals annually in the United States, making them the largest human-influenced source of mortality for birds and mammals in the country.

Cats are not villains. When they prey on wildlife they are simply following their instincts. Ecologically, however, the negative impact of this predation is undeniable and unnatural. As a species imported around the globe by humans, domesticated cats' negative impact on wildlife is an extension of our own impact on our environment and it is up to us to prevent it.

Keeping cats indoors isn't only better for wildlife, it's better for cats, too. Cats that roam outdoors are killed by vehicles, disease, or predators such as coyotes and live much shorter lives than indoor cats. According to the Humane Society of the United States cats that go outside often don't live to five years of age, while indoor cats typically live well into their teens.

Follow these tips to keep your pet cats safe and happy, and wildlife safe from cats:

- Keep your cat indoors and give it lots of love, attention, exercise, and mental stimulation.
- Hide treats throughout the house to encourage natural hunting and foraging behavior.
- Provide lots of toys and rotate them out to keep your cat interested.
- Put a bird feeder outside a window to give your cats safe bird-watching opportunities.
- Train your cat to walk on a leash for supervised outdoor excursions.
- Install a "catio," a screened-in outdoor enclosure that allows cats safe outdoor time.
- Always spay and neuter your pet cats to prevent new litters, and adopt your pets from the shelter to minimize the number of unwanted cats in your community.
- Provide plenty of cover for birds and other wildlife to stay hidden from neighborhood cats. Densely plant shrubs or build a brush pile.
- Place birdbaths and feeders, both of which are often targeted by hunting cats, no closer than ten feet from cover so birds can see potential predators.
- Motion detector lights or sprinklers can help deter outdoor cats from hunting on your property.

What to Do about Snakes

How do you eliminate snakes in your wildlife habitat garden? Mothballs and snake "repellents" are toxic and don't work to repel snakes, so don't waste your money. Mowing or cutting away all of the vegetation and brush in your yard removes important habitat for birds and other wildlife. So what do you do if you spot a snake? The answer is sit back and enjoy it. There's usually no need to eliminate snakes in your yard.

Snakes are perceived as "bad" because of deep-seated myths and phobias that are out of proportion to the potential danger they pose to us. Snakes are some of the most harmless—and most important—wildlife that we can attract to our gardens. In fact, the vast majority of snakes are 100 percent harmless to people and are important predators. Yet the most common reaction most people have when they see a snake is to want to kill it.

If a snake shows up in your yard, you are doing something right. **It's something to be celebrated.** It means that you've created a healthy ecosystem that is helping wildlife. Snakes are beautiful and important wildlife. Enjoy them!

Follow these tips to avoid any conflicts with snakes:

- Critter-proof your home by making sure all entry points have tight-fitting doors or windows. Caulk any cracks or crevices that might allow snakes to enter. Keep screens in windows and don't leave doors open. (See also page 33.)
- Keep brush or rock piles and dense vegetation away from the foundation of your house.
- Build brush or rock piles and plant dense vegetation on the outskirts of your property to attract snakes to those areas, away from your home.
- If you have rats or mice in your home, work to eliminate them as they can attract snakes looking for a food source.
- Never use cruel glue traps—for rodents or for snakes.
- Encounters with venomous snakes in backyards are rare. Learn what snakes are venomous in your area so you know which snakes are actually dangerous, and which are totally harmless.
- If you do encounter a venomous snake in your yard, don't try to move or kill it. Call a professional wildlife removal company with experience with venomous snakes, or just let it be if children and pets aren't present.
- Never deliberately approach any snake or try to touch or handle it, and you'll eliminate any chance of ever being bitten. This goes for all wildlife. Teach this rule to children.

Snakes are both predators and prey and an important part of the garden ecosystem.

Plants as Food

Wildlife species native to your area have evolved with plants that are also native to that area. The best way to provide food for wildlife is to restore native plant communities in your yard or garden. Plants provide food for wildlife in a variety of ways, including seeds, berries, fruit, nuts, nectar, pollen, foliage, and sap.

Plants produce most of these foods specifically to attract wildlife. For example, flowers are brightly colored and fragrant not for human enjoyment, but as a way of attracting bees, hummingbirds, butterflies, and other insects to the high-energy nectar within. (It doesn't hurt that we find them beautiful, too.) The nectar is offered by the plant as a lure for these specialized wildlife species, called pollinators, to get them to brush against the reproductive parts of the plant and transfer pollen from one flower to the next

Native plants provide nectar and pollen to native bees.

Butterflies coevolved with the plants native to their habitat and rely on them for food.

to fertilize it. Seventy-five percent of flowering plants require animal pollinators in order to successfully reproduce. The fruits, berries, and nuts that are produced by fertilized flowers are little more than tasty and nutritious packages for a plant's indigestible seeds. Animals digest the edible parts, pass the seeds through their digestive tracts, and deposit them far away from the parent plant, where they are ready to germinate. This relationship is a win-win for both native plants and native wildlife and an example of a balanced ecosystem in action.

White oak

Tupelo

Birch

Sassafras

NATIVE TREES AND SHRUBS THAT PROVIDE FOOD FOR WILDLIFE

Many different species of most of these types of trees and shrubs occur throughout North America. Native trees provide food for wildlife in the form of seeds, nuts, berries, and nectar, and are host plants for caterpillars. Those caterpillars and other insects are important food for birds and other wildlife. Visit *www.nwf.org/garden* for native plant resources.

- American beech (*Fagus grandifolia*)
- Aspen/cottonwood (*Populus* spp.)
- Beautyberry (*Callicarpa americana*)
- **Birch (*Betula* spp.)**
- Blackberry (*Rubus* spp.)
- Blueberry (*Vaccinium* spp.)
- Cherry (*Prunus* spp.)
- Crabapple (*Malus* spp.)
- Currant (*Ribes* spp.)
- Dogwood (*Cornus* spp.)
- Elderberry (*Sambucus* spp.)
- Fir (*Abies* spp.)
- Fringe tree (*Chionanthus virginicus*)
- Hackberry (*Celtis occidentalis*)
- Hawthorn (*Crataegus* spp.)
- Holly (*Ilex* spp.)
- Juniper (*Juniperus* spp.)
- Mountain ash (*Sorbus scopulina*)
- **Oak (*Quercus* spp.)**
- Oregon grape (*Mahonia* spp.)
- Pine (*Pinus* spp.)
- **Sassafras (*Sassafras albidum*)**
- Serviceberry (*Amelanchier* spp.)
- Spicebush (*Lindera benzoin*)
- Spruce (*Picea* spp.)
- Sumac (*Rhus* spp.)
- **Tupelo (*Nyssa* spp.)**
- Viburnum (*Viburnum* spp.)
- Wax myrtle/bayberry (*Myrica* spp.)
- Willow (*Salix* spp.)

NECTAR PLANTS FOR POLLINATORS

Pollinators such as bees and butterflies rely on nectar as a primary food source. Bees also collect pollen as a protein-rich food source for their young. Some plants produce nectar and pollen that is more attractive to these pollinating animals. Some bee species are actually specialists that rely on the pollen from only certain plants.

Here are some of the best native perennial wildflowers to support and attract pollinators:

- Alumroot (*Heuchera* spp.)
- Aster (*Aster* spp.)
- Aster (*Symphyotrichum* spp.)
- Beardtongue, penstemon (*Penstemon* spp.)
- Beebalm, wild bergamot (*Monarda* spp.)
- Bellflower (*Campanula* spp.)
- Black-eyed Susan, brown-eyed Susan (*Rudbeckia* spp.)
- Blanketflower (*Gaillardia* spp.)
- Blazing star (*Liatris* spp.)
- Bluebells (*Mertensia* spp.)
- Cardinal flower (*Lobelia* spp.)
- Clematis (*Clematis* spp.)
- Columbine (*Aquilegia* spp.)
- Coreopsis (*Coreopsis* spp.)
- Culver's root (*Veronicastrum* spp.)
- Dogtooth violet (*Erythronium* spp.)
- Evening primrose (*Oenothera* spp.)
- False indigo (*Amorpha* spp.)
- Gentian (*Gentiana* spp.)
- Goatsbeard (*Astilbe* spp.)
- Goldenrod (*Solidago* spp.)
- Goldentop (*Euthamia* spp.)
- Hibiscus (*Hibiscus* spp.)
- Hyssop (*Agastache* spp.)
- **Ironweed (*Vernonia* spp.)**
- Joe-Pye weed, boneset (*Eupatorium* spp.)
- **Lupine (*Lupinus* spp.)**
- Meadow Alexander (*Zizia* spp.)
- Meadowfoam (*Limnanthes* spp.)
- Milkweed (*Asclepias* spp.)
- Mountainmint (*Pycanthemum* spp.)
- Phlox (*Phlox* spp.)
- Pickerelweed (*Pontederia* spp.)
- Poppy (*Eschscholzia* spp.)
- Prairie clover (*Dalea* spp.)
- **Prairie coneflower, Mexican hat (*Ratibida* spp.)**
- Purple coneflower (*Echinacea* spp.)
- Rattlesnake master (*Eryngium* spp.)
- Rockcress (*Arabis* spp.)
- Senna (*Senna* spp.)
- Sneezeweed (*Helenium* spp.)
- Spiderwort (*Tradescantia* spp.)
- Spring beauty (*Claytonia* spp.)
- St. John's wort (*Hypericum* spp.)
- Stonecrop, Sedum (*Sedum* spp.)
- Sunflower (*Helianthus* spp.)
- Thimbleweed (*Anemone* spp.)
- Violet (*Viola* spp.)
- **Wild geranium (*Geranium* spp.)**
- Wild indigo (*Baptisia* spp.)
- Wild petunia (*Ruellia* spp.)

Prairie coneflower

Lupine

Ironweed

Wild geranium

Beebalm

Coral honeysuckle

NECTAR PLANTS FOR HUMMINGBIRDS

Columbine

Indian paintbrush

Over 160 North American native plants are exclusively dependent upon hummingbirds for pollination. In the east, the ruby-throated hummingbird is the only species that commonly occurs. It is very territorial and will chase others away from feeders and flowers, so scatter these resources throughout your property to avoid competition. The 14 western species of hummingbirds are less territorial and can be quite gregarious, and it's not an uncommon sight to find several different species sharing a single feeder.

Here are some North American native and nonproblematic non-native plants to attract hummingbirds:

- **Beebalm (*Monarda didyma*)**
- Cardinal flower (*Lobelia cardinalis*)
- **Columbine (*Aquilegia* spp.)**
- Coralbells (*Heuchera sanguinea*)
- **Coral honeysuckle (*Lonicera sempervirens*)**
- Fire pink (*Silene virginica*)
- Flowering tobacco (*Nicotiana* spp.)
- Fuchsia (*Zauschneria* spp.)
- Geiger tree (*Cordia sebestena*)
- **Indian paintbrush (*Castilleja coccinea*)**
- Jewelweed (*Impatiens capensis*)
- Mexican honeysuckle (*Justicia spicigera*)
- Penstemon (*Penstemon* spp.)
- Pineapple sage (*Salvia elegans*)
- Red buckeye (*Aesculus pavia*)
- Red yucca (*Hesperaloe parviflora*)
- Scarletbush (*Hamelia patens*)
- Scarlet morning glory (*Ipomoea cristulata*)
- Scarlet sage (*Salvia splendens*)
- Standing cypress (*Ipomoea rubra*)
- Sunset hyssop (*Agastache rupestris*)
- Tropical sage (*Salvia coccinea*)
- Trumpet creeper (*Campsis radicans*)
- Turk's cap mallow (*Malvaviscus arboreus* var. *drummondii*)

WILDLIFE PROFILE:
POLLINATORS

Pollinators are a diverse group of wildlife species that fertilize plants while moving from flower to flower in search of nectar, pollen, or nesting materials. Once fertilized, plant blossoms form berries, fruits, vegetables, and seed heads, which are critical food sources in the natural food web as well as for people. These pollination services are critical to agriculture—one-third of our food is the direct result of animal pollinators—as well as the health of natural ecosystems. Most pollinator species are also easily provided for in habitat gardens.

Many different kinds of wildlife serve as pollinators, including:

Bumble bee

BEES

With over 4,000 species native to North America, bees are our most important and efficient pollinators. They come in all sizes, from large carpenter and bumble bees to tiny sweat, mason, and leafcutter bees. Some have the classic black and yellow coloration, but others lack stripes and sport shiny green, black, or blue coloration. Bumble bees form hives but most native bees are solitary nesters, laying eggs in tunnels in the ground, in hollow plant stems, or in decaying wood. Honey bees are a domesticated species brought to North America by humans.

FLIES

Many fly species feed on flower nectar and act as pollinators. Syrphid flies—also known as hoverflies or flower flies—are some of the most effective pollinators, and many mimic bees with their black and yellow coloration. Unlike bees, they only have one pair of wings rather than two, and their eyes are large and meet at the top of their heads while bees have smaller eyes that don't connect. In addition to being pollinators, syrphid fly larvae are beneficial predators, feeding on pests such as aphids. Midges and even mosquitoes are other members of the fly family that feed on nectar and act as pollinators.

Syrphid flower fly

WASPS

Bees evolved from wasps, and like their bee cousins, many wasp species feed on flower nectar and serve as pollinators.

Great golden digger wasp

Unlike bees, most wasps are also predatory, patrolling the garden for other insects to feed their young. In doing so they act as important pest control.

BUTTERFLIES AND MOTHS

Butterflies and moths are some of our most visible pollinators. To attract these insects, plant nectar plants as a food source for adults (see page 46), and host plants for their caterpillars (see page 122). Some host plants are also valuable nectar sources, such as milkweed.

BEETLES

Many beetle species feed on flower nectar and pollen and in doing so act as pollinators. Species of long-horned beetles, scarab beetles, and the aptly named flower beetles are just some of the many pollinating beetles to look out for in your garden.

HUMMINGBIRDS

Hummingbirds love feeding at long, tubular flowers. This is no accident, but rather the result of coevolution. Tubular flowers are perfectly shaped to transmit pollen to the foreheads of these long-billed birds as they drink nectar from deep within the blooms. They transmit the pollen to the next flower they visit, fertilizing it.

BATS

Most bats in North America feed on insects, but two species—the lesser long-nosed bat and the Mexican long-tongued bat—feed on flower nectar from cacti such as saguaro and cardon, agave, and other night-blooming desert plants. Their long faces and brush-tipped, tubular tongues allow them to reach deep into the blossoms to get nectar. Their faces become covered with pollen in the process, which they pass on to the next flower they visit, fertilizing it. Excess pollen is groomed off and consumed as an added protein source, along with insects within the flowers. These bats also feed on cactus fruits. Each spring, they migrate north from Mexico into parts of Arizona, Texas, and New Mexico, and have even learned to use backyard hummingbird feeders.

Acmon blue butterfly

Longhorn beetle

Anna's hummingbird

Mexican long-tongued bat

Native Plant Specialists

Many wildlife species can feed on a variety of different types of plants. Some species, however, depend on specific types of native plants for survival, notably insects. Most plants produce toxins to keep insects from eating their leaves and stems. Over hundreds of thousands of years of coevolution, insects have developed a resistance to the toxins of select plants. As a result, ninety percent of insects that feed on plants can only survive on those that are native to their region.

For example, the caterpillars of butterflies and moths can only feed on certain plants, called "host plants." Some species have a wide range of host plants, while others can only feed on one type. Monarch butterfly caterpillars, for example, can feed only on milkweed (*Asclepias* spp.). Without the proper host plants, butterflies and moths can't complete their reproductive cycle and populations decline.

Similarly, between twenty and thirty percent of native bee species are also specialists. These bees only collect pollen to provision their young from certain plants, and without those plants in the landscape, populations of these bees disappear. Some native plants that support specialist native bees include blueberry, deerberry, and cranberry (*Vaccinium* spp.), willow (*Salix* spp.), goldenrod (*Solidago* spp.), asters (*Symphyotrichum* spp.), sunflowers (*Helianthus* spp.), dogwood (*Cornus* spp.), redbud (*Cercis candadensis*) and violets (*Viola* spp.).

Butterfly and moth caterpillars can only feed on certain plant species. Without these "host plants" in the landscape caterpillars can't survive and species disappear.

Almost all songbirds rely on insects as a primary food source for themselves or their young. This mountain bluebird has caught a cricket.

Bugs as Food

Native plants provide seeds and berries fed on by many species of backyard birds, but birds need more than just these plant foods to survive. Insects and other invertebrates are a critical protein source for almost all the songbirds you're trying to attract, along with woodpeckers, kestrels, screech and burrowing owls, quail, and even hummingbirds. Most feed their babies exclusively on these invertebrates, many of which themselves rely on native plants for their own survival. Most songbirds, for example, rely largely on moth caterpillars as food for their young. After caterpillars, spiders and then crickets are the most important groups of invertebrate food sources for birds.

And it's not just birds that feed on invertebrates. After native plants, invertebrates are the next most important food source for other wildlife in the food web. Amphibians such as frogs and salamanders eat them. Reptiles from turtles to lizards to snakes feed on them. Mammals do, too. Chipmunks, flying squirrels, white-footed mice, bats, opossums, skunks, ringtails, and even foxes rely on invertebrates for a significant part of their diets. Invertebrates eat each other, too. Dragonflies, mantids, ladybugs, and spiders are just a few of the predatory invertebrates that feed on other invertebrates.

What this all means is that if you want to attract birds and all of the other wildlife that rely on invertebrates as a key part of their diet, you need to attract these "bugs." Filling your garden with native plants and avoiding pesticides (see chapter 6) is the way to do that.

BUTTERFLY OR MOTH?

Butterflies and moths are closely related groups of insects that together make up the order Lepidoptera. Eighty to ninety percent of the lepidopterans are moths. That means most of the caterpillars that birds feed their young are moth caterpillars—something to consider when you're planning that "butterfly" garden (see page 123). Make sure to include host plants for moth caterpillars too if you also want to attract nesting birds.

Here are a few ways to tell the difference between butterflies and moths:

BUTTERFLIES	MOTHS
• When resting, butterflies fold their wings over their backs, perpendicular to the ground.	• When resting, moths typically fold their wings down along their sides, parallel to the ground.
• Butterfly antennae have rounded balls at the tips and are called club antennae.	• Male moths have feather-like antennae, while female moth antennae are smooth.
• Butterflies are active during the day.	• Moths are nocturnal and fly at night (although not all).
• Many butterflies are brightly colored.	• Many moths are duller shades of brown or gray, but there are a lot of exceptions. Some moths sport bright colors and are just as beautiful as butterflies.
• Butterfly bodies are slim and smooth.	• Generally, moths have stout, furry bodies. Many moth caterpillars are also furry or bristly.
• Butterflies pupate in a smooth capsule called a chrysalis.	• Many moth caterpillars spin a silken cocoon when they are ready to pupate.

A silver-bordered fritillary butterfly.

A polyphemus moth.

Food in All Seasons

You will have the most success in attracting a wide variety of wildlife to your yard or garden if you provide a mix of plants that together provide food throughout the year in all four seasons. This will ensure a steady availability of nectar, fruits, nuts, seeds, foliage, pollen, sap, and prey species throughout the year.

Plant a mix of native plants that bloom in different seasons, some in spring, some in summer, and some in fall. Not only will this ensure you have a beautiful garden throughout the seasons, it will mean you're offering nectar and pollen when butterflies, hummingbirds, bees, and other pollinators are active. Blooming wildflowers set seed in summer and fall after they've been pollinated. Many shrubs and trees that bloom in spring and early summer also provide berries in late summer and fall. Some keep their berries well

into winter. These seeds and berries are important food sources for birds and small mammals. This not only helps species that go dormant or hibernate in winter, which need to fatten up in the late summer and early autumn in order to survive winter, it also helps migratory species, which need a steady source of food over a wide geographic range in both fall and spring.

Monarch butterflies are one of the few migratory insects. They rely on late-blooming plants such as asters (*Symphyotrichum* spp.) and goldenrods (*Solidago* spp.) to provide the nectar they need to make their journey south to Mexico or Southern California. Winter-resident birds rely on berries from native plants such as holly (*Ilex* spp.), sumacs (*Sumac* spp.), Washington hawthorn (*Crataegus phaenopyrum*), and chokeberry (*Aronia* spp.) that persist into the winter.

Chokeberry in **spring**

Chokeberry in **winter**

Milkweed in **summer**

Milkweed in **fall**

Supplementing with Feeders

The best way to provide food for wildlife is to preserve and restore the local native plant communities that have supported them for thousands of years. However, you can use feeders to supplement the natural food you provide through native plants. Providing feeders is also a great way to observe wildlife at a close range at a regular location.

Feeders are a fun way to attract birds, such as this cardinal and blue jay, for easy viewing.

Bird Feeders

Studies have shown that birds rely on natural food sources first and use feeders only to supplement their diet. They won't become unnaturally dependent on feeders and won't delay seasonal migration or starve if you stop feeding them when you go on vacation. Instead they use feeders the same way they use a shrub that has put out berries: they feed on the berries until they're gone, then move on to other local food sources.

There are a variety of different types of bird feeders available. **Tube feeders** are popular and can be filled with a variety of seed types to attract different bird species. **Platform feeders** can be used for birds that normally forage on the ground and don't like to use a hanging feeder, such as mourning doves and many native sparrows. **Hopper feeders** have a roof and sides, typically hold a larger volume of seed, and often come in a variety of whimsical designs. **Sock feeders** made of fine mesh hold tiny seeds for birds such as goldfinches, while larger mesh can hold peanuts for species like blue jays, titmice, or Steller's jays. There are even feeders designed to hold dried insects or pieces of fruit for birds that don't normally eat seed or visit other types of feeders, such as bluebirds or orioles.

Always keep in mind that while some birds may use feeders, almost all species require insects as a source of food for themselves and their young. This is even true of hummingbirds, which can't survive on nectar alone. Only about twenty-five percent of bird species will even use a feeder. Make sure you provide diverse native plant communities to support the year-round food needs of the birds that occur in your area.

SUET FEEDERS

You can provide birds with a high-energy food source in winter by providing suet. Suet is

There are many types of bird feeders. Here a pileated woodpecker visits a suet feeder.

rendered, or melted, animal fat. Suet feeders are wire cages that allow birds to cling to the wires and peck at the suet.

Suet is typically sold in square blocks sized to fit in standard suet feeders, and it can be purchased with a variety of additives such as dried fruit, seeds, and even dehydrated insects. You can make suet yourself by getting raw beef fat from a butcher, melting it, and then cooling it. (Be warned: this can be a very smelly process.) Pour the rendered fat into a large glass casserole dish, add dried fruit, seeds, or nuts and let it cool and re-solidify. Then you can cut squares sized to fit into your suet feeder. Store suet in the freezer until you're ready to use it.

Woodpeckers, nuthatches, creepers, chickadees, titmice, and even hawks will eat suet if they can get it, especially in winter when other food sources are scarce. Other types of wildlife like suet as well. Tree squirrels and chipmunks will take advantage

Goldfinches feed on tiny Nyjer seed from a sock feeder.

A Baltimore oriole feeds on oranges and grape jelly. Feeders are a treat, not natural habitat.

of suet feeders, and the occasional raccoon, opossum, or fox may clean up the scraps that fall to the ground (if wildlife other than birds are regularly visiting your suet feeder, take it down so they don't become dependent on it).

NECTAR AND FRUIT FEEDERS

You can provide hummingbirds and other nectar-eaters such as orioles and some warblers with special feeders designed to hold sugar water "nectar." You can purchase nectar mix, or you can make your own by dissolving white sugar in water.

FRUIT FEEDERS

Many birds feed on wild berries and fruits, including robins, catbirds, mockingbirds, waxwings, some warbler species, and woodpeckers. Orioles in particular love to eat fruit. You can offer fruit "feeders" simply by placing berries in a tray feeder or any shallow dish and putting it out

OTHER BIRD FEEDER FOODS

- Mealworms
- Wax worms
- Raisins
- Currants
- Cherries
- Cranberries
- Grapes
- Grapefruit or orange halves
- Fruit jelly
- Peanut butter
- Sugar water "nectar"
- Popcorn

in your yard. You can also add grapes and orange halves to the dish, or hang these on tree branches or a shepherd's hook.

There are special feeders designed specifically to attract orioles that have a reservoir for sugar water nectar. These feeders have perches for orioles to land on since they cannot hover while feeding

BEST SEEDS FOR FEEDERS

Different seed types will attract different species of birds to your feeder. Use seed types that are appropriate for your feeders. Black-oil sunflower will be eaten with relish by almost any bird species that will visit a feeder. Safflower is less appealing to squirrels and to non-native birds such as English sparrows.

Black-oil sunflower	Striped sunflower	Sunflower hearts (hulled sunflower)
Safflower	Nyjer	Red millet
White millet	Cracked corn	Peanuts (whole, shelled, or pieces)

HOMEMADE NECTAR FOR YOUR HUMMINGBIRD FEEDER

To make homemade hummingbird nectar, boil one part sugar in four parts water. For orioles, boil one part sugar in six parts water. Be sure to let your homemade nectar cool before offering it to birds.

Be sure to only use white sugar. While not particularly healthy for humans, white sugar dissolved in water in the right concentration is a close simulation of the flower nectar fed on by wildlife. Don't use brown sugar and never use honey or artificial sweeteners. Honey spoils quickly when mixed with water and artificial sweeteners lack the calories the birds need to survive.

Empty and clean nectar feeders every two to three days, especially in warm weather, or the nectar can go bad and make birds sick. You can refrigerate a batch of nectar for up to a week. After that, discard it and make a fresh batch. Hummingbirds are attracted to the color red, and many hummingbird feeders are red for this reason. Adding red food dye to your nectar isn't necessary and could potentially harm the birds. Instead, use a red-colored feeder. Planting red, tubular flowers is the most natural way of providing food for hummingbirds.

like hummingbirds can. Oriole feeders often also have places for orange halves and bowls to offer fruit jelly. You can purchase special "oriole" jelly formulated to be less sweet than jellies made for human consumption, which have significantly more sugar than natural fruits, or simply dilute your favorite jelly with water.

MAMMALS AND BIRD FEEDERS

Anyone who feeds birds knows that squirrels will soon show up to get their share. Love them or hate them, squirrels at your bird feeders is usually an inevitability. Using a squirrel-proof feeder that humanely deters these small mammals can help. Models with a cage around them or that close their ports when a squirrel puts its weight on the perch work well. Baffles placed either above or below the feeder (or both) can also work. Many people eventually adopt the "if you can't beat 'em, join 'em" attitude and simply put out extra seed for the scampering rodents. If done in moderation this usually isn't a problem.

KEEPING SQUIRRELS OUT OF BIRD FEEDERS

- Use a baffle, which is a piece of plastic or metal, which blocks the squirrel from the feeder. If the feeder is on a pole, add a baffle underneath the feeder. If the feeder is hung from a branch or if squirrels can drop onto the feeder from above, add a baffle on top of the feeder.
- Use a feeder surrounded by caging that allows birds to get at the seed but blocks squirrels.
- Use a feeder that uses the weight of the squirrel to close seed ports. Birds will be light enough to use the feeder, but the weight of a squirrel will close the seed ports.
- Feed safflower seed instead of sunflower. Safflower is less palatable to squirrels but is relished by many birds.
- Don't put petroleum jelly or cooking oil on feeder poles to deter squirrels. These materials can damage fur or make squirrels ill.
- Learn to enjoy squirrels because no one has yet come up with a feeder or method that's perfectly squirrel-proof!

BIRD FEEDING TIPS

- Hang feeders in a spot that is easy to observe so you can enjoy the birds.
- Store seed in a dry place. Moisture can cause mold to grow, which can make birds sick.
- Clean feeders regularly to prevent disease. Scrub with a stiff brush and hot water or run through the dishwasher. Disinfect with a solution of one part bleach to nine parts water.
- Allow the feeder to dry completely before adding fresh seed.
- Keep the areas under the feeder raked clean. Seed shells and bird droppings can harbor disease and spilled seed could attract rats.
- Use feeders rather than spreading seeds on the ground, which can also attract pests.
- Don't overfeed. A few feeders are fine, but more than that can cause unnatural crowding that can cause stress and spread disease.
- If you have a problem with birds flying into your window, place the feeders closer to your house. Many birds hit windows when flying away from feeders.
- Prevent rodents or mold from getting into your seed supply by storing it in a metal bin with a tight-fitting lid placed in a cool, dry location.
- Keep feeders away from areas that provide cover for domesticated cats. If cats are staking out your feeders as hunting grounds, take the feeders down for a few weeks.
- Keep squirrels out of feeders (see page 59 for tips).

Unlike birds, when fed, mammals can lose their fear of humans and stop eating natural foods. Planting native plants is the best way to feed wildlife.

Beyond the occasional squirrel, however, you should never feed mammals. Unlike birds, mammals can become dependent on people for food and stop eating their natural diet, which is unhealthy and can lead to malnutrition. An even more serious consequence is habituation, when wild animals lose their natural fear of people. When mammals such as raccoons, foxes, deer, javelina, skunks, or bears associate us with food they begin approaching people looking for a handout—a potentially dangerous situation. Wild animals that do this often must be euthanized.

If mammals are getting into your trash, keep it indoors until the morning of collection. Don't feed pets outside because wildlife will take advantage of that food source, too. If mammals are visiting your bird feeders on a regular basis, the only responsible thing to do is to take the feeders down. The good news is that filling your yard or garden with native plants will provide both mammals and birds with natural food sources, both from the plants themselves as well as the smaller animals they support as part of the food chain.

FAMILY PROJECTS:
MAKE EASY BIRD FEEDERS

You can make a variety of fun feeders as an occasional treat for backyard birds. These edible feeders make great ornaments for your outdoor plants during holiday seasons or any time of the year. They are also great projects for kids.

WILDLIFE COOKIES

SUGGESTED MATERIALS:
- Cookie cutters (stars, animals, etc.)
- 1 loaf of white bread
- 1 roll of ribbon

1 Use cookie cutters to punch shapes out of bread. Create a variety of shapes. **2** Use a pencil to poke a hole at the top of each cut-out piece of bread for hanging. Leave the bread out overnight to harden. **3** Use ribbon or string to hang your ornaments outside around your yard.

Wildlife
Cookies

Pinecone
Feeders

Edible Garland

Bagels for the Birds

WILDLIFE ENERGY MUFFINS

SUGGESTED MATERIALS:

- 1 cup chunky peanut butter*
- 1 cup pure rendered suet or vegetable shortening
- 2½ cups coarse yellow cornmeal
- Seeds, raisins, or other dried fruit and roasted peanuts
- Pipe cleaners

1 Mix peanut butter, suet, and cornmeal together. Stir in seeds, fruit, and nuts. **2** Make "muffins" by placing the mixture into a muffin tin. Sprinkle seeds on top. **3** Place a pipe cleaner in each muffin to act as a hanger, and place the tin in the freezer to harden. **4** Once hardened, hang the muffins from a tree.

If tree nut allergies are an issue, use soy butter or tahini as an alternative.

PINECONE FEEDERS

SUGGESTED MATERIALS:

- 1 cup chunky peanut butter*
- 1 cup pure rendered suet
- 2½ cups coarse yellow cornmeal
- 1 bag birdseed
- 1 box of raisins
- 1 roll of ribbon

1 Tie a length of ribbon to the base of the pinecone. Mix together peanut butter, suet, corn meal, 1 cup of birdseed, and ½ cup of raisins in a small bowl. **2** Stuff the mixture into each pinecone. **3** Roll pinecones in additional birdseed. **4** Hang from trees with string or ribbon.

If tree nut allergies are an issue, use soy butter or tahini as an alternative.

BAGELS FOR THE BIRDS

SUGGESTED MATERIALS:
- 1 bag of plain bagels
- 1 jar of plain peanut butter*
- 1 bag of birdseed
- 1 roll of ribbon

1 Split bagels lengthwise and let them harden overnight. **2** Spread peanut butter over both sides of each bagel slice. **3** Sprinkle with birdseed. **4** Tie lengths of ribbon through each bagel hole and hang bagels throughout your backyard.

If tree nut allergies are an issue, use soy butter or tahini as an alternative.

GRAPEFRUIT FEEDERS

SUGGESTED MATERIALS:

- 1 grapefruit (or orange)
- 2 pounds of suet
- 1 bag of birdseed
- 1 roll of string or ribbon

1 Cut grapefruit in half and hollow out. **2** Poke three holes in the edge of the grapefruit half that you are going to stuff. Tie string or ribbon through the holes, leaving 1 foot or more for hanging. **3** Stuff suet into the hollowed-out grapefruit half. **4** Sprinkle birdseed on suet. Place in the freezer to harden; then hang in yard.

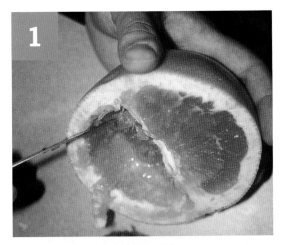

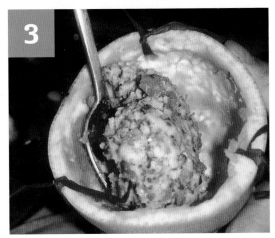

EDIBLE GARLAND

SUGGESTED MATERIALS:

- 1 roll of twine
- Sewing needles
- 2 bags of popped popcorn
- 3 bags of raw peanuts (in shells)

- 5 apples (cut into chunks)
- 2 bunches of grapes
- 2 bags of cranberries
- 4 oranges

1 Assemble all the ingredients before starting, and cut large pieces of fruit into sections. **2** Using the sewing needles, string items together, alternating between popcorn, apple chunks, grapes, cranberries, raw peanuts, and anything else you want to include. **3** Drape your garland around an evergreen tree or shrub. You can attach orange segments with red ribbon as highlights.

If tree nut allergies are an issue, use soy butter or tahini as an alternative.

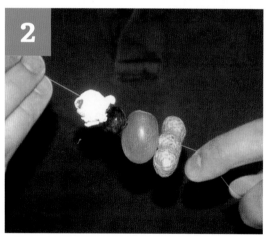

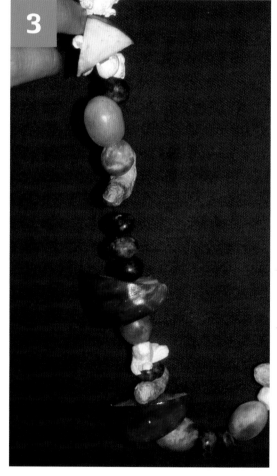

Red-spotted purples are butterflies that enjoy feeding on the juices of overripe fruit.

Butterfly Feeders

Not all butterflies feed on flower nectar. Some species prefer tree sap, fermenting fruit, and even animal manure or carrion that liquefy as they decompose and offer sources of nutrient-rich food. This is especially true of woodland butterfly species like wood satyrs, wood nymphs, commas, question marks, and mourning cloaks. Even those butterfly species that do feed on flower nectar will sometimes take advantage of these other food sources.

You can create a special kind of feeder for butterflies. Begin by filling a shallow dish with chopped pieces of fruit such as bananas, grapes, melon, apples, or pears. Fresh fruit works but those that are overripe and beginning to get a bit mushy are even better. Mash the skin so that the fruit oozes out. Place the fruit in a shallow dish out in your garden on the ground or on top of a stump. An empty birdbath works well. To make the fruit feeder even more attractive to these winged beauties, you can add a splash of sugar water, sports drink, beer, rum, or wine. (Remember, butterflies naturally consume fermenting fruit in the wild.)

As with bird feeders, if mammals such as raccoons, foxes, or bears are eating the fruit from your butterfly feeder, take it down.

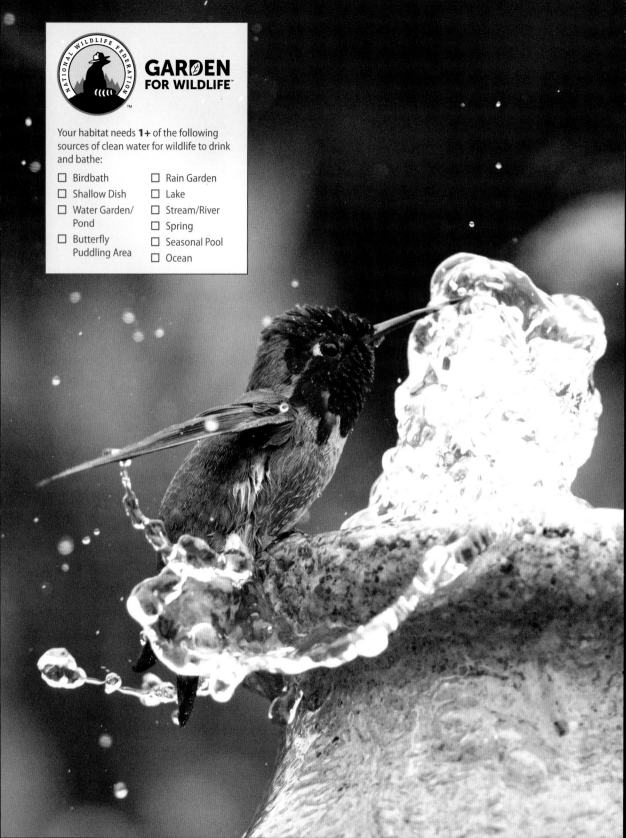

GARDEN FOR WILDLIFE™

NATIONAL WILDLIFE FEDERATION

Your habitat needs **1+** of the following sources of clean water for wildlife to drink and bathe:

☐ Birdbath
☐ Shallow Dish
☐ Water Garden/ Pond
☐ Butterfly Puddling Area
☐ Rain Garden
☐ Lake
☐ Stream/River
☐ Spring
☐ Seasonal Pool
☐ Ocean

CHAPTER THREE

Water

All wildlife species need water for drinking and birds need water for bathing as well. If birds can't bathe, their feathers become dirty, making flight difficult. Some species feed on aquatic or semiaquatic prey. In addition, water provides cover for a variety of wildlife, and many species need water to reproduce and as a place for their young to grow.

A water source in the garden is a magnet for wildlife.

There are many ways you can provide water in a wildlife habitat garden. Options range from large ponds to simple birdbaths. Even a muddy puddle will provide certain wildlife with this necessary habitat element. Different species of wildlife use water in different ways. What kind of water features you choose will determine the types of wildlife you'll attract.

For example, a large pond might attract herons and other wading birds or waterfowl such as ducks and geese, along with aquatic turtles, muskrats, or even beaver. A smaller water garden might become home to frogs or used as a breeding place for salamanders and dragonflies. A birdbath won't attract these kinds of wildlife, but songbirds will love it, and if you place the bath on the ground, or create a wetland garden, so will ground-dwelling animals.

If you are planning to add a water resource to your yard, mimic the ways water would naturally occur there. This is important not only because local wildlife have adapted to use water in the way it naturally occurs but also because providing water in unnatural ways can have negative ecological consequences. Water features that are out of place where you live, such as a large pond in the middle of the desert, can support invasive non-native species, draw potentially dangerous wildlife close to your home, or be a wasteful use of this important resource.

Birdbaths

There are many styles of birdbaths. The best baths are relatively shallow. One to three inches is best. A birdbath that is too deep won't be as usable for small birds. You can place pebbles or one larger rock in the birdbath to allow birds and insects a place to land to get a drink. A bath made of plastic will be easier to move and clean, but will deteriorate more quickly out in the elements.

Any shallow dish can become a water source for birds, insects, and other wildlife.

FAMILY PROJECT:
MAKE A BIRDBATH STUMP

You can create a simple, naturalistic water feature with nothing more than an old tree stump. Either a stump that is still rooted in the ground or a large log will work. You will also need a sharp chisel and some plants and rocks for the base of the birdbath stump.

Your stump birdbath will become a focal point in the garden as well as a water resource for birds and other wildlife. Empty the birdbath every few days and refill with fresh water to eliminate mosquitoes.

Be careful to place your birdbath in an area near cover for birds to hide in should a domesticated cat or other predator appear, but not so close that these predators can use the cover to ambush birds and other critters coming for a drink. A distance of 10 to 12 feet is ideal.

1 If you're using a log, pick one that has a flat top and bottom and is at least 15 inches in diameter. Stand the log up on one end. An adult should use the chisel to tap out chunks of wood from the top of the log. The depression should be about 3 inches deep or less. Don't worry about making the depression smooth. Birds actually prefer a birdbath with rough surfaces, which keeps them from slipping when they land to drink or bathe.

2 If the stump is large enough, add a rock on which birds can land, or place pebbles in the bottom of the depression. You can change the pebbles whenever you wish. Visually anchor your stump with a few large stones at its base, and plant native ground cover. Alternately, you can simply place a shallow bowl of water on top of the stump.

BIRDBATH MYTHS

Birds naturally get water in the winter by consuming snow or from moving streams, and they have no problem surviving without heated water provided by humans. Providing unfrozen water simply makes it easier for birds to get liquid without expending the extra body heat needed to melt snow. Feathers and feet will not freeze if they get wet in a birdbath.

Concrete, glass, and metal are also good choices, but they may be heavy and difficult to move, and concrete can crack in freezing weather. Glazed ceramic is an excellent choice, being relatively light, easy to clean, and attractive.

Shallow Water Dish for Ground Critters

Most birdbaths are made to sit on a pedestal, hang from a hook or branch, or attach to the railing of a deck or balcony. You can also place your birdbath directly on the ground. Any shallow dish placed on the ground will provide water for birds but also for wildlife that can't fly or climb, such as toads, rabbits, or tortoises. You can place a branch over the dish for a perch or create a small rock pile adjacent to the dish for critters to bask and hide. The dish itself will serve as a hiding place for insects and other invertebrates, as you'll learn when you lift it for cleaning and see the many small creatures

Placing a birdbath on the ground provides water for animals that don't fly or climb, like this striped skunk.

scurrying for cover. These smaller wildlife species are a food source for birds and other insectivorous wildlife.

Birdbath dishes taken off their stand, flowerpot drainage dishes, or even plastic trash-can lids buried upside down can be used to create ground-level water features that will attract wildlife.

Ponds, Water Gardens, Puddles, and Rain Gardens

Ponds and water gardens are popular features that will be used by a variety of wildlife species. Ponds can be large, natural bodies of water or smaller features that you create. Water gardens include smaller natural ponds, but the term also refers to container gardens that hold water, such as half-barrels or even old bathtubs and water troughs.

CREATE OR PRESERVE UNDERWATER HABITAT

Below the surface of the water, the branches of fallen trees create a maze of chambers and crevices for hiding and hunting. Freshwater fish and other aquatic species use these areas of fallen woody debris in much the same way that oceanic species use coral reef structures and terrestrial creatures use brush piles. Fallen woody debris also slows the current, which prevents erosion and creates resting, feeding, and hiding places for aquatic species. For example, the removal of fallen woody debris from many Pacific Northwest streams and rivers has proven disastrous for several salmon species that need the slower-moving pools that such areas create as safe hiding and feeding places for young. If you have fallen woody debris in your body of water, leave it in place. If no woody debris is present, consider adding a large log, a fallen snag, or even a tangle of branches.

Ponds

Natural, earth-bottomed ponds allow the maximum opportunity for natural plant growth, and they offer places for wildlife to hibernate in the mud and debris at the bottom. But in most places, if you simply dug a hole and filled it with water, the water would seep into the ground. Even in areas with high clay content soils, water will eventually percolate down. To prevent water from being absorbed, you'll need to install either a preformed hard plastic pond, or use a flexible plastic pond liner.

BUILD A WILDLIFE POND

TOOLS & MATERIALS

- 1 garden hose, or spray paint
- Shovels, picks, and other digging tools
- 1 4-foot level
- 1 straight 2 x 4 long enough to span hole
- 1 pool liner and pond pump
- Pond plants

1 Pick a location for your new pond. Use a garden hose to outline the area where you'd like the finished pond to be. You can use spray paint to "draw" the outline as well. The depth of the pond will depend on your region and which wildlife species you wish to attract. The colder the climate, the deeper the pond needs to be to accommodate aquatic wildlife year-round. In most places a depth of 30 inches is sufficient to ensure that the pond doesn't freeze entirely, killing fish, hibernating reptiles, amphibians, and other aquatic wildlife. Extremely cold areas will require a depth of 4 feet.

2 Plan the underwater topography by sketching a cross section of what you want your pond to look like underwater. Plan for a variety of levels and shelves at different depths. Include a wide, shallow area on one side that will allow wildlife such as amphibians to enter and exit easily. Birds will also use the shallow section to drink and bathe. Sketching your ideas on paper before actually digging will allow you to experiment with different designs. Once you've settled on a design plan, determine the specific depth and slope of each shelf to guide you as you dig.

3 The shape of your wildlife pond should be natural and undulating instead of rigid and symmetrical. Use a level and a 2 x 4 to ensure that the perimeter is level from edge to edge, otherwise water will spill out of the lower side. Once you've dug the hole according to plan, carefully rake the soil in the hole as smoothly as you can, removing any rocks or other jagged debris that could potentially tear the liner. Adding a layer of smooth sand as a buffer is a good idea as well.

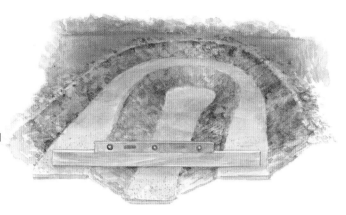

4 Unroll the liner in a warm, sunny spot to make it more pliable, and then place it over the hole. Press it against the ground in the hole with your hands, molding it to the shape of the shelves. There will be some wrinkles and creases that look unattractive in the empty pond, but once the pond is filled with water and plants, you won't be able to see them. Be sure to overlap the liner at least 8 inches around the edge of the pond to prevent the water from draining under the liner if the pond floods during a heavy rain. Place decorative rocks around the edge to hide the liner and hold it in place.

5 Add a pump and plants, and then sit back and wait for the wildlife to arrive. It won't be long! You can also jump-start your pond ecosystem by adding a couple bucketfuls of water and leaf debris from a nearby pond. Make the shoreline more accessible to wildlife by placing stacked rocks, logs, or branches that dip into the water. These will be used by wildlife as "ladders" to enter and exit the pond. Native vegetation in and around the pond will also help wildlife get in and out, and it will provide food, cover, and places to raise young as well. Aquatic plants need to be potted, since they will not be able to root themselves into the plastic liner.

Water Gardens

Water gardens can be created using any number of containers to hold water and plants. When creating water gardens, keep wildlife use in mind. Water troughs, half-barrels, or any other container with steep sides and that is deeper than three inches can trap wildlife that falls into the relatively deep water, unless vegetation or some other exit point is provided. Songbirds typically won't use this type of water feature either. You can make your water garden more wildlife-friendly by adding potted water plants or branches or even by adding large rocks to serve as "islands."

PUMPS AND FILTERS

It's a good idea to invest in a pond pump to circulate and aerate the water. Attach plastic tubing to create a waterfall, which will add an element of sound. Birds, in particular, are attracted to the sound of moving or trickling water. Many different-sized pumps are made specifically for garden ponds. They are rated by the number of gallons they'll pump in the span of an hour. At a minimum, you'll need a pump that will circulate all the water in your pond in that hour. The bigger the pond, the bigger the pump you'll need. If you don't have an electrical outlet nearby, you'll need to work with an electrician to install a GFCI outlet, which is the type necessary for outdoor locations. For smaller ponds, you can try a solar powered pump that won't require any electrical work. You might want to also add a filter. Again, get a filter rated for the size of your pond.

Puddles and Muddy Areas

You can create another type of water feature that might seem a little strange: a mud puddle. Butterflies can often be seen engaging in a behavior called "puddling." When they find a wet, muddy patch of soil, they gather and suck up the muddy liquid, which is rich in minerals. If you don't have a naturally muddy spot in your yard, you can create your own puddling area by filling a shallow dish with a mix of sand and compost mixed with water until just muddy, but without pools of standing water to keep mosquitoes from breeding, and placing it in a sunny area.

In addition to being used by butterflies as a place to get a drink of mineral-rich water, many bee and wasp species as well as birds such as robins, barn swallows, and phoebes will collect the mud to build their nests.

Butterflies drink the mineral-rich water from muddy soil.

Wetland plants such as these pitcher plants thrive in wet soil.

Wetlands and Rain Gardens

Wetlands are areas that hold shallow, standing water and occur naturally where the topography of the land causes water to collect and pool. There are many different types of natural wetlands. A swamp is a wooded wetland. A marsh is a wetland that does not support trees and is characterized by grasses, sedges, rushes, and other herbaceous plants adapted to full sun, saturated soils, and standing water. Vernal pools, wet meadows, wet prairies, and prairie potholes are all types of wetlands that collect standing water from precipitation but typically dry out during the summer or dry season. A bog is a type of wetland in which plant material has accumulated faster than it can decompose and formed a substrate called peat. Bogs are usually very acidic and poor in nutrients. Native carnivorous plants, such as sundew (*Drosera* spp.), pitcher plant (*Sarracenia* spp.), butterwort (*Pinguicula* spp.), and Venus flytrap (*Dionaea* spp.) grow in bogs. Their ability to lure and trap insect prey as a nutrient source is an adaptation to living in nutrient-deprived bogs.

You can create your own wetland garden by mimicking natural wetlands. You can divert storm runoff from your roof or from a basement sump pump into an area planted with wetland species. You can also plant wetland species in any area that naturally collects water in your yard. A rain garden is a type of wetland garden that mimics a natural wet meadow or prairie. Rain gardens are planted in a location specifically to absorb water and nutrients that would otherwise wash off your yard into storm drains after it rains. There are native plants adapted to wet conditions in most regions that will thrive in a wet area in your yard. Wetland gardens like these will provide wildlife habitat and reduce runoff.

FAMILY PROJECT:
CREATE A RAIN GARDEN

A rain garden is a special type of wetland garden designed to absorb rainwater. When it rains, large amounts of water can run across the landscape, causing erosion and washing excess fertilizer and other pollutants into the storm drains at high speed. This polluted, fast-rushing water shoots from the storm drain right into the local stream, eroding the banks, causing siltation and destroying habitat. A rain garden acts as a sponge, sucking up the rainwater and nutrients before they hit the storm drain.

1 Choose a site for your rain garden based on the flow of water across your property. The rain garden should be situated away from the house at the point where water runs off the property or in a low-lying spot. Sunny spots work best, as most wetland plants require full sun.

2 Outline the area for the rain garden, remove the sod, and dig out the soil to about 14–18 inches deep. If the property is sloping, use some of excavated soil to build a berm on the low side to keep water from running off.

3 You can also direct the water running off your roof to the rain garden by attaching a flexible plastic pipe to your downspout and burying it in a trench leading to the rain garden. Only do this with larger rain gardens to ensure that all the runoff water can be absorbed.

4 Backfill the hole with a mixture of two-thirds existing soil and one-third compost. If your soil is very clayey, discard the existing soil and refill with a mixture of sand and compost. Gradually slope the sides with the lowest point in the very middle.

5 Fill your rain garden with native wetland plants that provide food, cover, and places to raise young for wildlife, with the most water-tolerant species at the lowest point in the middle.

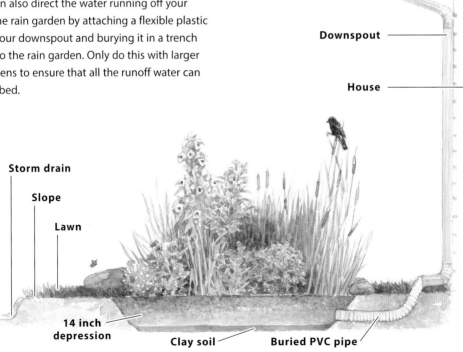

Roof

Downspout

House

Storm drain

Slope

Lawn

14 inch depression

Clay soil

Buried PVC pipe

BULLFROGS IN THE WEST

The American bullfrog is native to the eastern and central parts of the United States and Canada. It has been widely introduced outside its range, however, and has become a problematic invasive non-native species in the West. It consumes other frogs such as the endangered Chiricahua leopard frog native to Arizona, New Mexico, and Mexico.

Never purchase and release into the wild tadpoles or frogs from mail-order science supply catalogs or from pet shops. Chances are that they are not native to your area, and they could become invasive or spread disease to wild populations. A better way to experience these creatures is to create habitat and let native amphibians come on their own.

Buffer Zones for Shorelines

Moving bodies of water such as streams or creeks provide habitat for different wildlife species than those found in ponds or lakes. If you have a moving water feature naturally occurring on your property, protect it from erosion and runoff with a buffer of native vegetation.

If you're lucky enough to own property adjacent to a large, natural body of water, whether it's a lake, river, stream, or coastal area, maintain natural vegetative buffers that protect the water from runoff of silt from erosion, as well as from chemical fertilizers and pesticides. In addition to protecting these bodies of water, buffer areas provide habitat for a variety of creatures.

Leave a riparian zone, a swath of vegetation 10 to 12 feet wide, along the shoreline of natural bodies of water. Don't remove fallen logs or other woody debris that extend from the shoreline, which provide an important basking area for turtles and other semiaquatic reptiles and amphibians. They are also used as hunting perches by wading birds.

ADD A MOVING-WATER FEATURE

If your property has a slope, you can create your own moving water feature using the same types of pump and flexible plastic liner that you'd use to create a small pond. Build a small pond area at the bottom of the slope, and then run flexible piping to the top of the slope. Dig a long, curving "stream-bed" depression, and line it with flexible pond liner. Cover the streambed with gravel and randomly placed larger stones, and add streamside plants. Finally, pump the water from the lower pond up to the top, where it will run down the streambed and create a wonderful moving water habitat.

Don't mow all the way down to the water's edge. Allow native plants to grow to absorb runoff and provide wildlife habitat.

Logs along the shoreline of larger water bodies serve as important basking habitat for pond species such as these painted turtles.

Maintaining Your Water Feature

While you're deciding on the type of water source you'd like to provide for wildlife, consider the amount of maintenance that will be required to keep it clean. If you allow your water source to become dirty, it could be harmful to wildlife. Smaller, shallower water sources can easily be polluted by animal waste and need to be emptied and washed often. In ponds and water gardens, plants provide habitat for wildlife, but they also serve as natural filters of animal waste and excess nutrients. Purchasing a pump-driven filter is also an option.

Dealing with Algae

Algae blooms often occur in newly established ponds. This is a normal part of the process as microorganisms develop that will become the "biological filter" for the pond. Once established, aquatic vegetation will outcompete algae for light and nutrients and prevent excessive algae blooms. It normally takes new ponds six to eight weeks to find their balance once other plants are added. Monitor nutrient load in the pond to prevent continued algae blooms. Don't let any fertilizer get into the water from the surrounding landscape. If you must fertilize aquatic plants, use pellets designed for that specific purpose. Don't overstock your pond with fish, and don't overfeed them because fish waste and uneaten food promote excess algae. Organic barley straw or straw extract and natural beneficial bacteria purchased from a garden center or online can be added to the pond to reduce algae blooms without the use of synthetic chemicals.

Once your pond is established, allow a moderate amount of dead leaves and debris to accumulate on the bottom. These areas will be used as breeding and hiding places for aquatic invertebrates as well as reptiles, amphibians, and amphibian larvae. If your pond is deep enough and has enough submerged debris, some amphibian and reptile species may also use it as a hibernation area.

Dealing with Ice

Birds and other wildlife will eat snow in winter, but that requires additional heat energy from their bodies to melt it into liquid form. When temperatures are below freezing and liquid water is frozen, but there is no snow on the ground, there is literally no available liquid water for wildlife. Make sure wildlife has liquid water available year-round by emptying ice out of birdbaths or shallow water dishes each morning and refilling with tepid water that will take a while to refreeze. You can also use a birdbath heater, which keeps the water just above the freezing point and can be a real bird magnet in freezing temperatures.

For small ponds, it's important to keep part of the surface ice-free throughout winter. A solid layer of ice will trap gases in the water, which can kill overwintering fish and amphibians. Moving water takes longer to freeze so adding a waterfall will help keep the surface partially ice-free, especially in areas with milder winters. For areas that reach freezing temperatures during winter for more than a few days, a pond heater is necessary, which will melt a hole on the surface of the ice to allow gas exchange. The most effective are electric and can be plugged in where you plug in your pond pump. Solar-powered pond heaters are also available.

Eliminating Chemicals from the Water

Birds, reptiles, amphibians, and other aquatic wildlife are extremely susceptible to chemical pollutants. Be careful what you put on your lawn and garden, because fertilizers and pesticides may wash into your water feature and kill wildlife.

Even if you don't use chemicals in your yard, you might be adding them when you top off your pond. In most municipalities chlorine or chloramine is added to tap water to kill microorganisms that could be unhealthy for humans. Both can harm fish, amphibians, and the microorganisms in the water. Chlorine evaporates out of tap water within twenty-four hours but chloramine persists much longer. In areas with just chlorine in the water, simply filling a bucket with hose water and aging it for a day or two will allow the chlorine to evaporate out. In areas with chloramine, purchase water conditioner from a pet shop or water-garden supply company that will neutralize both chlorine and chloramine instantly.

Controlling Mosquitoes

Biting mosquitoes are a nuisance and they can also spread diseases such as the West Nile and Zika viruses. Wearing long sleeves and using repellents

Heaters keep ice from totally covering small water gardens, allowing gases to escape.

can minimize bites, but you can go a step further by preventing mosquitoes from breeding in your wildlife habitat garden in the first place.

Eliminate breeding spots. Mosquitoes can lay eggs in standing water. Look for standing water in clogged gutters, drainpipes, children's toys, plant saucers, and tree cavities. Empty or remove these water sources.

Maintain water features. It takes mosquitoes five to ten days to complete metamorphosis from aquatic larvae to winged adults. To keep mosquitoes from reproducing in your birdbath, simply dump the water out—along with any eggs and larvae—every few days. Mosquitoes prefer to lay eggs in stagnant, still water so add a waterfall or fountain to ponds to keep the water surface moving.

Don't spray. Resist the urge to broadly spray pesticides over your yard. Research has shown

SHOULD YOU BUY EXOTIC FISH?

Goldfish and koi are domesticated non-native fish that are not always a great fit for a natural water feature for wildlife. While they will eat mosquito larvae in your pond, they will also feed on wildlife such as dragonfly larvae and frog and salamander eggs and larvae. Koi and goldfish are native to Asia, and in some cases when they've escaped or been released from captivity, these non-natives have had a negative impact on native wildlife. If you do have such exotic fish, be sure that they have no means of escape into natural waterways, and never deliberately release these species into the wild. In addition, choosing such fish for a pond in a wildlife-friendly landscape could be an unwise investment; koi in particular are very expensive and so brightly colored that they are often an easy catch for native fish predators like herons and raccoons.

WILDLIFE PROFILE:
TOADS

Toads are wonderfully lumpy and bumpy creatures that should be welcomed into your wildlife habitat garden. Toads are really just a specific group of frogs, generally characterized by dry, bumpy skin, stubby legs, blunt snouts, and a preference for walking rather than hopping. These adaptations allow toads to be more terrestrial than other frogs, and many toads spend time in the water only for mating, preferring to burrow into the ground or hide in the vegetation for cover. Toad "warts" are not warts at all. They are actually glands that produce foul-tasting secretions that deter predators.

Toads are important backyard predators. Like most amphibians, they will eat anything that moves and is small enough to fit in their mouths. They relish slugs and insect pests and, for this reason, make excellent garden inhabitants.

To attract toads, provide cover in the form of low-growing plants and a nice thick layer of mulch or, even better, leaf litter, in your garden beds. Brush piles, fallen logs, or even a clay or ceramic "toad abode" will also provide hiding places (see page 110). Avoid pesticides, which kill the insects that toads feed upon and can even kill the amphibians themselves. If you install a garden pond, you might even be rewarded with the trills of breeding toads in the springtime.

Dragonflies prey on mosquitoes as both winged adults and as aquatic larvae.

that this is not very effective at reducing mosquito populations and that it can kill beneficial insects. Focusing on larval control is much more effective.

Use natural larval control. In addition to eliminating standing water, you can also inoculate water with a natural soil bacterium that kills mosquitoes called *Bacillus thuringiensis* (Bt). The Bt strain *israelensis* kills the larvae of mosquitoes, fungus gnats, and biting blackflies but is harmless to people as well as other wildlife. You can get Bt *israelensis* in the form of doughnut-shaped mosquito "dunks" or in granule form from garden centers, hardware stores, or online.

Nurture mosquito predators. Both adult mosquitoes and larvae are on the menu for a wide variety of wildlife, from birds and bats to frogs, lizards, fish, and dragonflies. Planting native plants and taking other steps to support these predators can minimize the local mosquito population.

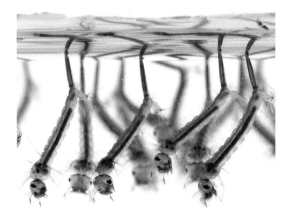

Reduce mosquitoes by eliminating breeding places for their larvae.

GARDEN FOR WILDLIFE™

NATIONAL WILDLIFE FEDERATION

Your habitat needs **2+** of the following places for wildlife to take shelter from the weather and predators:

- ☐ Wooded Area
- ☐ Dense Shrubs/ Thicket
- ☐ Bramble Patch
- ☐ Meadow/Prairie
- ☐ Evergreens
- ☐ Ground Cover
- ☐ Brush/Log Pile
- ☐ Rock Pile/Wall
- ☐ Burrow
- ☐ Cave
- ☐ Roosting Box
- ☐ Water Garden/ Pond

CHAPTER FOUR

Cover

Wildlife needs places to find shelter from extreme hot and cold temperatures, high winds, storms, and other weather conditions. Wild animals also need hiding places to escape predators. At the same time, predators rely on cover to camouflage and conceal themselves in order to successfully catch their prey.

There are a variety of ways that wildlife finds cover in the wild, so there are many different ways you can provide it in your yard or garden.

A barred owl finds shelter from the wind in the hollow of a dead tree.

Plants provide the best cover for wildlife. Evergreens offer cover year-round.

Plants as Cover

In the same way that native plant communities provide the best and most sustainable food source for wildlife, they also provide the best form of cover. Because wildlife species evolved with native plant communities, their life cycles and cover needs are in tune with the seasonal changes of native plants. Any native plant community will provide natural cover for the wildlife species that are also native to the region.

Different native plants offer different types of cover. Plants that have dense growth patterns provide more cover from both weather and predators. Plants that have thorns on their leaves or branches add yet another layer of protection that will help smaller creatures enact a safe escape from larger predators. Evergreen plants provide excellent cover year-round, and

are particularly important in areas subject to cold temperatures.

No matter which plants you choose, providing cover is just as much about *how* you plant as it is about *what* you plant. The key to providing cover is to plant densely and in a way that mimics the natural structure that native plants form in the wild. For example, forest plant communities have several different structural "layers," from the forest floor all the way up to the treetop canopy. Each of these layers supports different wildlife species. If you have large mature trees, add an understory layer of smaller tree species and large shrubs. This understory can then be underplanted with smaller shrubs, woodland wildflowers, sedges, and ferns. In doing so, you provide several new layers of cover and will support many more wildlife species.

Butterfly bush

Burning bush

Scotch broom

Multiflora rose

INVASIVE NON-NATIVE SHRUBS TO AVOID

The following non-native shrubs and small trees are invasive in parts of North America and should not be planted. Most are still commonly available for sale in nurseries. In the past, some were touted for their wildlife value because some birds will feed on their berries. But when birds eat the fruit, they also spread the seeds, allowing these shrubs to invade and degrade diverse native plant communities that support many other species of wildlife.

- Amur honeysuckle (*Lonicera maackii*)
- Autumn olive (*Elaeagnus umbellata*)
- Brazilian pepper (*Schinus terebinthifolius*)
- **Burning bush (*Euonymus alatus*)**
- **Butterfly bush (*Buddleia davidii*)**
- Chinese privet (*Ligustrum sinense*)
- Cotoneaster (*Cotoneaster* spp.)
- European buckthorn (*Rhamnus cathartica*)
- European privet (*Ligustrum vulgare*)
- Glossy buckthorn (*Rhamnus frangula*)
- Japanese barberry (*Berberis thunbergii*)
- Japanese privet (*Ligustrum japonicum*)
- Japanese spirea (*Spiraea japonica*)
- Morrow honeysuckle (*Lonicera morrowii*)
- **Multiflora rose (*Rosa multiflora*)**
- Nandina/heavenly bamboo (*Nandina domestica*)
- Russian olive (*Elaeagnus angustifolia*)
- **Scotch broom (*Cytisus scoparius*)**
- Tartarian honeysuckle (*Lonicera tatarica*)

Black elderberry, nectar

Eastern red cedar, evergreen, berry

Inkberry, evergreen, berry

Black elderberry, berry

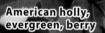
American holly, evergreen, berry

Mountain laurel, nectar

TIPS FOR PLANTING A NATIVE WILDLIFE SHRUB ROW

A wildlife shrub row is a densely planted row of woody plants made up of a variety of different native species. Wildlife species will hide within and use this "living fence" as a sheltered path as they move across the landscape.

- Select shrubs with varying mature heights to add visual interest.
- Select plant species that have flowers or berries that wildlife can use as food sources.
- Plant densely to provide the most cover, but keep the mature size of your plants in mind to limit overcrowding. For medium-sized shrubs, planting about 5 feet apart is good spacing.
- Use your shrub row to connect two naturally planted or wild areas that are separated by lawn or other open space. Your shrub row will then be used as a corridor.
- To provide the most cover, allow your shrubs to grow according to their natural branching structures rather than pruning them back or into geometric shapes.
- If you have bird feeders or birdbaths, place them about 10 to 12 feet from your shrub row. This is close enough that birds can escape to the shrub row if a cat appears but not so close that the cat will be able to use the shrub row as a hiding place from which to ambush the birds.
- A wildlife shrub row planted along your property line will also serve as a fence and privacy screen.
- Plant diversely to provide for the widest range of wildlife. **A good native shrub row recipe is one evergreen species, two nectar-producing species, two berry-producing species, and one thorny species.** The quantity of each species depends on available space.
- Plant native wildflowers and grasses in front of your shrub row to add more habitat and create a finished look.

Prairie rose,
thorny bush

Black chokeberry,
berry

Holly,
evergreen,
nectar

Wax myrtle/
southern bayberry,
berry

Salal,
nectar

Blueberry,
nectar

Muhly grass, or hairawn muhly, is native to the eastern and southern United States.

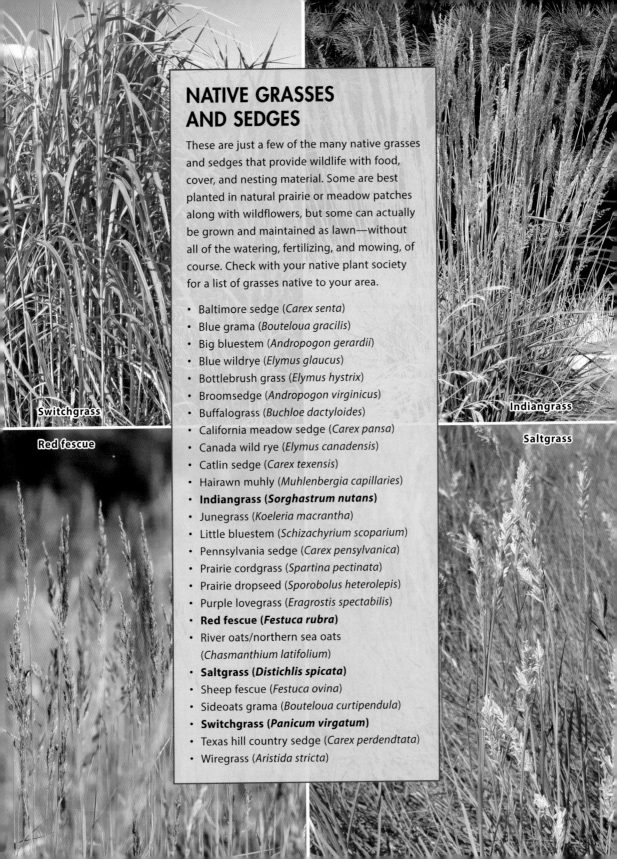

NATIVE GRASSES AND SEDGES

These are just a few of the many native grasses and sedges that provide wildlife with food, cover, and nesting material. Some are best planted in natural prairie or meadow patches along with wildflowers, but some can actually be grown and maintained as lawn—without all of the watering, fertilizing, and mowing, of course. Check with your native plant society for a list of grasses native to your area.

- Baltimore sedge (*Carex senta*)
- Blue grama (*Bouteloua gracilis*)
- Big bluestem (*Andropogon gerardii*)
- Blue wildrye (*Elymus glaucus*)
- Bottlebrush grass (*Elymus hystrix*)
- Broomsedge (*Andropogon virginicus*)
- Buffalograss (*Buchloe dactyloides*)
- California meadow sedge (*Carex pansa*)
- Canada wild rye (*Elymus canadensis*)
- Catlin sedge (*Carex texensis*)
- Hairawn muhly (*Muhlenbergia capillaries*)
- **Indiangrass (*Sorghastrum nutans*)**
- Junegrass (*Koeleria macrantha*)
- Little bluestem (*Schizachyrium scoparium*)
- Pennsylvania sedge (*Carex pensylvanica*)
- Prairie cordgrass (*Spartina pectinata*)
- Prairie dropseed (*Sporobolus heterolepis*)
- Purple lovegrass (*Eragrostis spectabilis*)
- **Red fescue (*Festuca rubra*)**
- River oats/northern sea oats (*Chasmanthium latifolium*)
- **Saltgrass (*Distichlis spicata*)**
- Sheep fescue (*Festuca ovina*)
- Sideoats grama (*Bouteloua curtipendula*)
- **Switchgrass (*Panicum virgatum*)**
- Texas hill country sedge (*Carex perdendtata*)
- Wiregrass (*Aristida stricta*)

Switchgrass

Red fescue

Indiangrass

Saltgrass

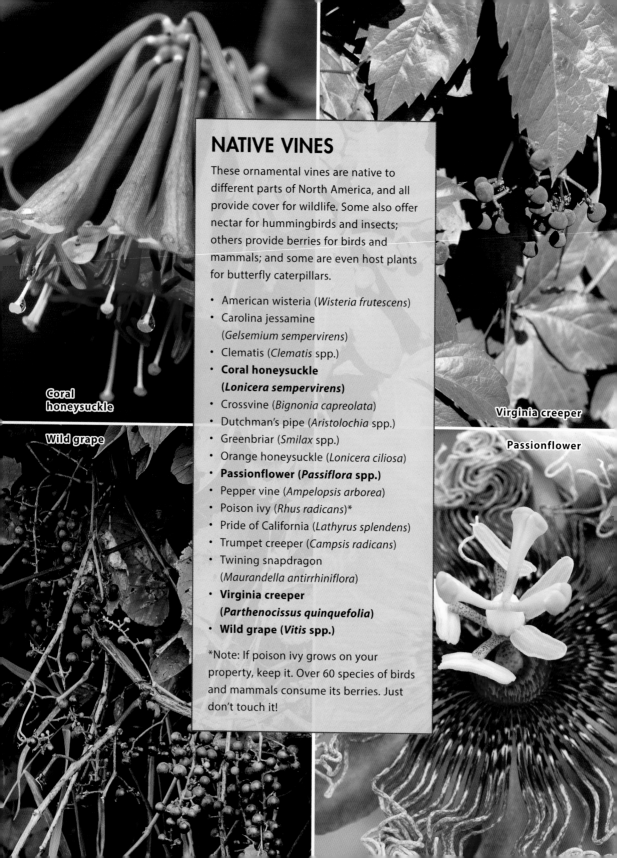

NATIVE VINES

These ornamental vines are native to different parts of North America, and all provide cover for wildlife. Some also offer nectar for hummingbirds and insects; others provide berries for birds and mammals; and some are even host plants for butterfly caterpillars.

- American wisteria (*Wisteria frutescens*)
- Carolina jessamine (*Gelsemium sempervirens*)
- Clematis (*Clematis* spp.)
- **Coral honeysuckle (*Lonicera sempervirens*)**
- Crossvine (*Bignonia capreolata*)
- Dutchman's pipe (*Aristolochia* spp.)
- Greenbriar (*Smilax* spp.)
- Orange honeysuckle (*Lonicera ciliosa*)
- **Passionflower (*Passiflora* spp.)**
- Pepper vine (*Ampelopsis arborea*)
- Poison ivy (*Rhus radicans*)*
- Pride of California (*Lathyrus splendens*)
- Trumpet creeper (*Campsis radicans*)
- Twining snapdragon (*Maurandella antirrhiniflora*)
- **Virginia creeper (*Parthenocissus quinquefolia*)**
- **Wild grape (*Vitis* spp.)**

*Note: If poison ivy grows on your property, keep it. Over 60 species of birds and mammals consume its berries. Just don't touch it!

Coral honeysuckle

Virginia creeper

Wild grape

Passionflower

English ivy

Chinese wisteria

Japanese honeysuckle

Kudzu

INVASIVE NON-NATIVE VINES TO AVOID AND REMOVE

Many commonly occurring vines are invasive non-native species. Some were accidental introductions, but most were brought to North America as ornamentals or for erosion control. Do not purchase these species, and try to remove those already in the landscape:

- Asian bittersweet (*Celastrus orbiculatus*)
- **Chinese wisteria (*Wisteria sinensis*)**
- Climbing euonymus (*Euonymus fortunei*)
- **English ivy (*Hedera helix*)**
- Fiveleaf akebia (*Akebia quinata*)
- **Japanese honeysuckle (*Lonicera japonica*)**
- Japanese wisteria (*Wisteria floribunda*)
- **Kudzu (*Pueraria montana*)**
- Mile-a-minute (*Polygonum perfoliatum*)
- Porcelainberry (*Ampelopsis brevipedunculata*)

Restore Grassland

Grassland plant communities provide excellent cover for a wide range of wildlife species, from insects and birds to small and large mammals. In grassland communities, grasses and wildflowers grow in dense, intermingled patches, sometimes with occasional trees and shrubs, with not one individual plant surrounded by bare soil.

Grasslands naturally occur over a wide range of the North American continent, from the southwestern desert grasslands of California and the Southwest, to the sagebrush steppe in the Intermountain West, to the prairie communities of the Great Plains. While forests have returned in many places, native grasslands have largely been converted ino agricultural land or, increasingly, to water-thirsty lawns composed of exotic grass species. Over ninety percent of America's grasslands are gone. As a result, grassland birds and monarch butterflies that rely on these ecosystems on their migratory routes are facing steep declines. Even a small patch of native grasses and wildflowers will provide great cover for a variety of creatures.

Dead Plants Are Full of Life

Even dead and dying plants can provide cover. After the flowers and leaves have died back, leave the dead stems of herbaceous plants standing until spring. The fruits and seeds that develop from flowers will become a food source, while the stalks provide an extremely important cover source for a

Fallen logs and branches provide excellent cover for a variety of wildlife.

A green anole lizard hides in the vegetation. When densely planted, your garden plants provide the essential habitat component of cover.

variety of insects. These insects that shelter in dead plant stems become an important food source for birds.

Similarly, fallen woody debris such as rotting logs on the ground or fallen branches provide an important source of cover for insects and other invertebrates, birds, small mammals, salamanders, lizards, and turtles. Dead standing trees are called "snags" and are an extremely valuable source of cover. As trees age, branches break off and holes begin to form. These cavities are used by many birds and mammals as important nesting areas as well as for cover. Leave snags standing in the landscape whenever possible, as long as they pose no danger of falling and injuring people or damaging property. Rather than completely removing the snag as decay progresses, you can minimize any potential hazard by pruning off the more rotten limbs or even the entire top portions. You can dress up a snag by planting native flowering vines at its base.

Leave the Leaves

Good news: it's okay to leave fallen leaves where they fall. Not only do fallen leaves provide a natural fertilizer as they break down and return their nutrients to the soil, they are their own mini-ecosystem that provides cover to small wildlife. Earthworms, snails, spiders, millipedes, and sow bugs are just a few of the invertebrates that hide out in the leaf litter. These creatures are food for chipmunks, salamanders, toads, moles, shrews, snakes, and terrestrial turtles that also hide out in the leaf litter, hiding from larger wildlife that prey upon them. Many animals overwinter under the leaf layer, from wood frogs, lizards, and box turtles, to many butterflies, moths, and even some bat species. Birds from wild turkeys to quail to wood thrushes forage for seeds, invertebrates, and other small wildlife living in the leaf litter.

WILDLIFE PROFILE:
BOX TURTLES

Box turtles are often the first reptile we see in the wild as children. Two US species—the common box turtle of the east and the ornate box turtle of the central and western states, both with several subspecies—can often be found living alongside humans in rural and suburban areas. Though they resemble tortoises with their domed shells and nonwebbed feet, box turtles are actually part of the pond turtle family. Despite this, they are wholly terrestrial.

These land-dwelling turtles have domed shells and often bear striking orange or yellow patterns on a dark olive-brown background that provide excellent camouflage in their woodland and grassland habitat. Their lower shell is hinged, allowing box turtles to seal their heads and front legs safely inside their shell to protect against predators, which is the source of their name.

Box turtles are omnivores, feeding on earthworms, slugs, snails, insects, carrion, mushrooms, berries, and green vegetation. To attract and support them in your wildlife habitat garden, plant densely to provide plenty of cover for these shy turtles and leave a thick layer of leaf litter where they can hide and forage. Native plants provide berries, fruits, and greens as well as support the invertebrates upon which box turtles feed.

Natural Cavities

Natural cavities can be found in rock or in the ground just as they are found in trees. These cavities are an important source of cover for many species of wildlife and should be protected and preserved. The many species of chipmunks and mole salamanders find cover in natural crevices and tunnels below the ground. Some mole salamander species emerge from these places for only a few days a year to mate, and then return underground. Filling in natural dens and burrow sites can evict many species of wildlife that depend upon them. Woodchucks, black-tailed prairie dogs, and the endangered gopher tortoise all excavate tunnels in the ground that many other wildlife species need as a source of cover.

Prairie dogs dig their own burrows for shelter.

Tree cavities offer cover for birds such as this tree swallow.

Bullfrogs and other aquatic amphibians dive beneath the water to find cover from predators.

Water as Cover

Water is the second natural way of providing cover for wildlife. Many creatures, in particular reptiles and amphibians, need bodies of water at least a few feet deep in order to escape predators. Green frogs, bullfrogs, southern pig frogs, and western spotted frogs are just a few of the species that dive into the water and hide in the mud and leaf litter at the first sign of danger.

Basking freshwater turtles also dive for the protective cover of water, and stay submerged until the danger has passed. Painted turtles, western pond turtles, and the many species of map turtles, river cooters, and sliders are common species that

exhibit this behavior. Some turtle species spend most of their time hiding below the water's surface and rarely leave their aquatic cover except to lay eggs. Musk turtles, snapping turtles, and spiny softshell turtles all behave this way. All of the frogs and turtles mentioned also use water as a source of cover to ambush their prey, which includes insects, fish, other amphibians and reptiles, and for the larger species, even birds and small mammals.

By adding or restoring water features to the landscape, you'll be providing cover for a great range of aquatic and semiaquatic species— predators and prey alike.

Constructed Cover

You can also construct or purchase landscape features that provide cover for wildlife. These human-made cover features replicate forms of cover that occur naturally.

Brush Piles

You can create the type of cover that naturally occurs when trees fall and dead wood accumulates on the ground by building a log or brush pile. Log piles are simply stacks of cut wood. If you have a fireplace, you probably already have a log pile that's providing hiding places for many small animals. Brush piles are made up of a variety of different sizes of wood and are less formal looking than a log pile. When built correctly, a brush pile can house creatures as large as foxes and as small as insects such as the mourning cloak butterfly, which will hibernate as an adult in a brush pile. Birds such

as wrens find both cover and places to hunt their insect prey in brush piles, and may even nest there. Building these woody wildlife hotels is also a great way to keep fallen yard debris out of the landfill.

Be sure to check with your homeowners' association or municipality to find out whether there are any ordinances against having brush piles, and don't build brush piles in areas where fire risk is high or in urban areas where they could harbor rats.

Rock Features

Rock piles offer excellent cover for wildlife. A rock pile can be as small or as large as you like, depending on the space and the rock with which you have to work. As with a brush pile, start with larger rocks at the bottom of the pile and add progressively smaller pieces. You can add a piece of

Stack fallen branches on the edge of the garden to create a brush pile to shelter wild creatures.

FAMILY PROJECT:
CREATE A BRUSH PILE

Although they may look like random piles of sticks and logs, if you build brush piles according to a specific plan you'll provide better cover for wildlife.

1 Place fireplace-size or larger logs on the ground about 12 to 15 inches apart. This will allow spaces for larger wildlife. Then take smaller branches, up to about 2 inches in diameter, and start crisscrossing them on top of the larger pieces.

2 Continue stacking wood in this manner. Add evergreen branches toward the top of the pile to add even more cover. Leave an opening or two toward the base. If you're concerned about the look of the brush pile, plant a flowering vine to grow over the top of it.

3 The finished brush pile should be about 5 feet in diameter at the base, shaped like a dome with larger cavities in the interior near the bottom, and with a maze of progressively smaller spaces toward the outside of the pile.

FAMILY PROJECT:
BUG HUNTING

Here is a great way for kids to learn about the tiny creatures that inhabit your wildlife habitat garden. Bury a clean metal can, such as a coffee can, so that the top of the can is even with ground level. Add a piece of fruit to the can. Place some stones around the opening, and lay a flat piece of wood over the stones. The opening should be just large enough to allow insects and other invertebrates to crawl into the can. The smell of the fruit will attract them. Check the trap each day. Use a field guide to identify and learn about the critters you've captured. For safety's sake, don't handle them, because some species can bite or sting. Don't keep the critters for more than a few hours, and always release them where you found them. The project is fun for adults, too.

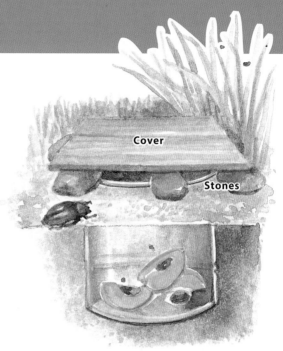

Adapted from Ranger Rick® *magazine.*

Rock walls are filled with crevices where small animals can find cover.

metal duct in the interior of your rock pile to create larger tunnels hidden by the exterior rock. Or create a rock wall. Like shrub rows, rock walls will serve as places of escape for wildlife as well as sheltered corridors across the landscape. If you build a rock wall, don't use mortar, which fills in all the spaces wildlife will use as cover. Simply stack the stone.

Rock features are particularly attractive to creatures that depend on their surrounding environment for temperature regulation. If you place your rock feature in a sunny area, it will absorb heat during the day and slowly release it during the cool evenings. Reptiles, such as skinks or horned lizards, and many butterfly species will bask in the morning sunlight after a chilly night or absorb heat radiating from the rocks in the evening as temperatures drop. In desert landscapes, rock features can play an important role from a landscape design perspective, adding visual interest and regional character.

Critter Houses as Cover

There are a variety of houses designed to provide cover for specific wildlife or groups of wildlife. Some critter houses are made commercially and can be purchased at your local garden store, at nature centers, or through catalog companies. You can also build critter houses from simple materials that you can purchase at a home-improvement center. You may even be able to recycle materials you already have.

Roosting Boxes

Roosting boxes provide protection for birds and small mammals during cold or harsh weather. By congregating together in the enclosed space of a roosting box, animals such as bluebirds or flying squirrels benefit from the collective body heat and the protection from bitter winds.

Roosting boxes look similar to nesting boxes, with a few key differences. The entry hole of a

Roosting boxes mimic natural tree cavities and give birds a place to sleep on cold nights.

roosting box is found at the bottom of the front side, which allows the box to retain heat in cold weather, as heat rises. Inside, roosting boxes often have a series of perches to accommodate up to a dozen birds. Roosting boxes can also be oriented either vertically or horizontally.

Different species use roosting boxes at different times of the year, so be sure to take the time to observe what is coming and going from your roosting box—you wouldn't want to miss a special wildlife viewing opportunity.

Burying lengths of pipe provides shelter for burrowing owls and other ground-dwelling species.

FAMILY PROJECT:
INSTALL A BAT BOX

Well-designed bat boxes that are installed properly will attract some species of bat. Many bats need surprisingly warm temperatures inside a bat box (anywhere from 85 to 100 degrees), so mount yours in an area that receives a lot of sun. In northern areas, stain your bat box dark brown to help it retain heat. Attach the box 15 or 20 feet off the ground. In order to fly, most bat species jump from their perch, drop, and then spread their wings. If your bat box is mounted too low, bats won't have the space they need to drop and take flight and therefore won't move in. Attach bat boxes to the side of the building or on poles. Those attached to trees give predators such as raccoons or snakes easy access and typically go unused by bats.

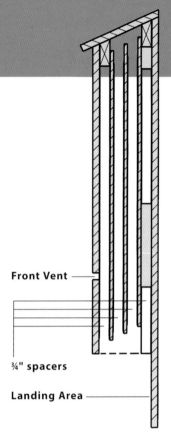

Front Vent

¾" spacers

Landing Area

COMMON BATS THAT USE BAT BOXES

These bat species commonly use properly mounted bat boxes as a source of cover.

- Little brown bat
- Big brown bat
- Mexican free-tailed bat
- Pallid bat
- Long-eared myotis
- Southeastern bat

Bat Houses

There are more species of bats in the world than any other group of mammal. Forty species can be found in North America and with the exception of two—the lesser long-nosed bat and the Mexican long-tongued bat of the desert southwest, both of which feed on flower nectar—they all feed on insects. Insect-eating bats play a key role in the ecosystem by consuming millions of insects every night, some of which are pests, and in the case of the nectar-eating species, by serving as pollinators.

Bats are nocturnal, flying at night to find food. During the day they need a safe place to roost, hidden from the elements and predators. Some species roost in caves, but many others find cover in tree cavities or even under loose pieces of bark. Bat boxes can mimic these valuable roosting places and attract these beneficial animals to your wildlife habitat garden.

Butterfly houses (above) and insect hotels (below) offer cover for a wide variety of insects.

Butterfly Houses

Butterfly houses mimic the natural crevices under tree bark, in brush piles, or spaces under leaves where butterflies naturally find cover from the elements. While there's no guarantee butterflies will use them, butterfly houses can add a nice decorative touch to a garden design.

Insect Hotels

Special structures designed to offer cover to a wide variety of insects and spiders are called "insect hotels." Generally multistory and rectangular in shape, insect hotels are comprised of multiple chambers that are filled with a variety of materials attractive as hiding places for invertebrates, including pine cones, bunches of dried grasses or twigs, hollowed-out stems of herbaceous plants, dead leaves, stacked lengths of cut branches, crushed rock, or clay pots. Insect hotels can add a rustic charm to your wildlife habitat garden and serve as a great source of cover for many tiny creatures.

A "toad abode" is a whimsical way to add a cover source for toads and other small critters.

Amphibian Houses

You can also make a critter house designed for the special needs of amphibians such as frogs, toads, and salamanders. You can purchase a decorative "toad abode" or make one on your own by recycling an old clay flowerpot. Simply use a hammer to crack off a small section of the lip of the pot; then place it in a shady part of your yard, upside down. The clay pot will help retain humidity and provide a cool, dark place for moisture-loving amphibians to find cover from the drying sun and from predators as well. Add a shallow water dish nearby to make the house more attractive to these amphibians. The drainage dish of the clay pot or even an old pie pan will work perfectly.

FAMILY PROJECT:
CREATE AN AMPHIBIAN HOUSE

In addition to a toad abode, you can create a house that will be used by terrestrial frogs, toads, and salamanders. Most amphibians have sensitive skin and need to find moist, dark cover from the sun. You can accomplish this using some scrap plywood and material you find around your yard. Just be sure to select a shady spot that is surrounded by cover. You can also include additional cover in your overall design.

1 Select a piece of scrap plywood or other wide piece of untreated lumber. The larger the piece of plywood, the more cover will be provided by your amphibian house. Select a shady spot near water; dig a 2 inch deep depression that is the same dimension as your piece of plywood. Place several fist-sized rocks in the corners of one side of the depression as shown in the illustration. The tops of the rocks should stick out over the top of the depression by at least 1 inch.

2 Lay the piece of plywood over the depression. One end should lie flat on the ground in the depression. The other end should be propped up on either side by the rocks, creating an entry point for amphibians and other wildlife.

3 Cover the plywood with several inches of mulch or old leaves, and plant native wildflowers or shrubs around the perimeter for added cover. For a multilayer cover feature, build a brush pile on top of the amphibian house. Place a water dish nearby.

NATIONAL WILDLIFE FEDERATION

GARDEN
FOR WILDLIFE™

Your habitat needs **2+** of the following places for wildlife to engage in courtship behavior, mate, and then bear and raise their young:

- ☐ Mature Trees
- ☐ Dead Trees/ Snags
- ☐ Meadow/ Prairie
- ☐ Dense Shrubs/ Thicket
- ☐ Nesting Box
- ☐ Water Garden/Pond
- ☐ Wetland
- ☐ Burrow
- ☐ Cave
- ☐ Host Plants for Caterpillars

CHAPTER FIVE

Places to Raise Young

All wildlife species need places to bear or raise their young. Providing food, water, and cover helps individual animals survive, but without adequate space and resources to find a mate and engage in courtship behavior, places and materials to build nests or dig dens and burrows, or the resources needed during the juvenile phase, wildlife populations will eventually decline. You can help make a difference for wildlife in your region by providing this important habitat component.

Creating safe places to give birth and raise young gives wildlife a future.

Natural Nesting Places

In the same way plants provide the best sources of food and cover for wildlife, they also provide a diverse array of wildlife with the resources necessary for reproduction. Wildlife will use many of the same places that provide cover—mature trees, densely planted shrubs or meadows, brush piles, tree snags—as places to raise young. The plants in your wildlife habitat garden will provide space and raw materials for nesting, egg-laying, or birthing for a diversity of wildlife from songbirds to butterflies to mammals.

Birds, for example, build nests hidden in the vegetation on the ground or in the branches of trees and shrubs, while others nest in tree holes, called cavities. Species that construct nests use plant stems and fibers as building material. No matter what the preferred nesting place is for backyard birds, they all rely on vegetation for

successful reproduction. Similarly, many insects lay their eggs in or on plants. Butterflies, moths, and many native bees rely on specific plants as a food source for their larvae (see page 50).

Native plants are the best choices for nesting places and egg-laying. Non-native plants can have

Some birds nest in branches like mourning doves, while others nest in cavities like this Gila woodpecker.

WILDLIFE PROFILE:
SCREECH OWL

Tiny screech owls are the perfect "backyard-sized" owl. At just four to six inches tall, they look like miniature great horned owls with their feather "horns," which the owls use for display to communicate with other owls. There are two species, the eastern and the western screech owl, and two color morphs within those species, the gray phase and the rusty-brown red phase.

Screech owls live in wooded areas and are happy to live in close proximity to humans, even in backyards and urban parks, provided there are enough mature trees to offer cover, nesting places and prey. Like all owls, screech owls are expert nocturnal predators. They feed on everything from insects to rodents and even other birds.

Attract screech owls by planting native trees and preserving existing ones on your property and by protecting woodlots throughout your community. Avoid insecticides and rodenticides, which kill their prey and could even poison screech owls themselves. Screech owls are cavity nesters and will happily lay their eggs in nesting boxes built and mounted to their specification. You might even catch them using a birdbath—just make sure to look outside at night!

a negative impact on the ability of wildlife to raise their young. One six-year study of an area near Chicago found that invasive non-native shrubs such as Amur honeysuckle (*Lonicera maackii*) and European buckthorn (*Rhamnus cathartica*) have given predators easier access to American robin and wood thrush nests than the locally native shrubs and trees traditionally used by these birds, including viburnum (*Viburnum* spp.), hawthorn (*Crataegus* spp.), maple (*Acer* spp.), and rough-barked hop hornbeam (*Ostrya* spp.). Monarch butterflies have declined due in large part to the elimination of their only caterpillar host plant, milkweed (*Asclepias* spp.) In fact, over ninety percent of native insects cannot complete their life cycles without native plants, which in turn robs parent birds of the most important food source for their young.

The only host plant for monarch butterfly caterpillars is milkweed.

Songbirds have better nesting success in native plants.

A red-headed woodpecker excavates a nesting cavity in a tree snag.

Nesting in Snags

Living plants are a critically important resource when it comes to places to raise young, but so are dead plants. In addition to providing much-needed cover, both snags (standing dead trees) and fallen woody debris provide important places for many wildlife species to raise their young. Insects burrow into the wood and form nests or egg chambers. Many insect species spend their larval phase in dead wood and become important food sources for creatures higher on the food chain. Many cavity-nesting birds and mammals, including squirrels, raccoons, and fishers, use holes in snags as nesting or birthing areas. Woodpeckers actually excavate cavities in declining trees and snags, and the cavities are then used by many other cavity nesters. Many birds and mammals will also nest or den inside a brush pile. Others will use the smaller twigs and branches from a brush pile as a source of materials for nest building.

Other cavity-nesting birds, such as this kestrel, use old woodpecker nesting cavities.

WILDLIFE PROFILE:
RED FOX

Red foxes are the largest fox species found in North America, and one of the most widespread, found coast to coast. Weighing in on average at just around fifteen pounds, red foxes are only slightly larger than the average housecat, just with longer legs and thicker fur. Despite their name, red foxes often have coats with gray, silver, or brown in them, and some are wholly dark. One thing all color phases of red fox have in common is a white-tipped tail.

Red foxes are intelligent and adaptable and are one of the few wildlife species that has expanded its range as humans have developed the landscape. Part of their success is due to their wide diet. Red foxes are omnivores, feeding on everything from mice, squirrels, and birds to grasshoppers and cicadas to fruits, berries, and grasses.

In early spring red foxes dig a den (or take over an old groundhog burrow) where the female gives birth to a litter of kits. The male participates in the raising of the offspring, hunting for the family. Though shy and elusive, red foxes can happily live alongside humans and pose no threat to pets or people, sometimes even denning right in our backyards.

Never feed red foxes, which causes them to lose their natural fear of people. Instead, plant a wide variety of native plants to provide natural sources of food and cover.

Groundhogs give birth to their babies in underground burrows.

Nesting in Burrows

Many mammals give birth to their young in burrows. Prairie dogs, ground squirrels, chipmunks, and groundhogs all dig underground burrows where they give birth. So do weasels and mountain beaver. Red foxes often take over old groundhog burrows while swift foxes dig their own from scratch. Allow these animals to engage in their natural burrowing behavior.

Gopher tortoises dig long underground burrows that dozens of other species use.

Native Bee Nesting

In North America, there are over 4,000 species of native bees. This doesn't include honey bees, which are a domesticated species imported from Europe for their agricultural pollination services and honey production. Honey bees, bumble bees, and some sweat bees live in social hives, but most other native bee species are solitary. This means they don't make honey or share in the care of their young. Instead, females of solitary bee species lay their eggs in a series of chambers in a nesting tunnel. These solitary nesters roll pollen and nectar into in a ball called "bee bread" or a "bee loaf" and lay one egg on it. They build a chamber wall and repeat the process until the tunnel is filled. Each egg hatches, the bee larva feeds on the bee loaf, pupates, and eventually chews out of its chamber as an adult to begin the process anew. While individual bees will nest in close proximity to each other where nesting conditions are favorable, they do not live communally.

Seventy percent of our native solitary nesting bees use tunnels they dig in the ground to lay their eggs. The other thirty percent use hollowed-out plant stems or tunnels made by termites, beetle larvae, and other insects (or woodpeckers drilling to get at those insects) in dead trees or fallen logs as egg-laying places. Some, such as carpenter bees, excavate their own nesting tunnels in decaying wood.

Providing nesting places for native bees is as important as providing native plants to supply them with pollen and nectar. Often, it's not the availability of flowers and nectar that limits bee populations in an area but rather the availability of appropriate nesting sites. Leave patches of bare soil in your garden for ground-nesting bees, leave plant stems standing through the winter, and keep dead trees or fallen logs. You can also put up "native bee nesting houses" filled with replaceable nesting tubes that provide places for native bees to reproduce.

Most bees don't form hives. They are solitary nesters. Females lay eggs in tunnels in the ground, in hollow plant stems, or in dead wood.

FAMILY PROJECT:
BUILD BEE NESTING HOUSES

You can create a nesting place that will be used by a variety of native bees. Orchard mason bees (*Osmia lignaria* and related species), which are important pollinators of both native plants and agricultural crops, will be attracted to and use bee nesting houses. Individual female native bees will use the tunnels in these nesting houses to lay a series of eggs, each of which is supplied with a ball of pollen and nectar known as "bee bread" to serve as a food source for their larvae.

Place the bee house on the south side of the building, fence post, or tree so that the house receives sun for most of the day. Once you've placed a bee house, do not attempt to move it until November when nesting activity has ceased.

1 Cut 8 to 10 dried plant stalks into 6-inch pieces. Using a drill, hollow out the stalks. **2** Tie the plant stalk pieces in a bundle and hang it in a sunny spot, or place them in a coffee can, plastic pipe, or rectangular wooden "house" mounted to a fence or building. **3** Replace the plant stalk pieces each year to prevent parasites from accumulating and killing bee larvae.

A gulf fritillary caterpillar feeds on its only host plant, passionflower vine.

Host Plants for Butterflies

Butterflies and moths are also important pollinators, and both require specific plants, called host plants, for their caterpillars to grow. Butterflies and moths have evolved very closely with the native plants of their region, and most rely solely on a small group of plants as food sources for their young. In some cases, the butterfly or moth caterpillar can eat only one type of plant. Without the appropriate host plant for these pollinators, you will not be providing a complete habitat for these lovely insects.

BUTTERFLY HOST PLANTS

BUTTERFLY SPECIES	CATERPILLAR HOST PLANT
• Monarch	• Milkweed (*Asclepias* spp.)*
• Tiger swallowtail	• Willow (*Salix* spp.)
• Mourning cloak	• Elm (*Ulmus* spp.)
• Gulf fritillary	• Passionflower (*Passiflora* spp.)*
• Question mark	• Hackberry (*Celtis* spp.)
• Buckeye	• Plantain (*Plantago* spp.)
• Wood nymph	• Purple-top grass (*Tridens flavus*)

These species are specialists that rely exclusively on these host plants.

FAMILY PROJECT:
PLANT A BUTTERFLY GARDEN

You can provide for adult butterflies simply by planting a garden full of nectar-providing plants. If you want a true butterfly garden, however, you'll need to provide for caterpillars as well. Start with a sunny location with low wind.

- Select a sunny location that you can easily see from your house, deck, patio, or other viewing area.
- Provide cover nearby with shrubs or perhaps a brush pile. A densely planted shrub row will also act as a windbreak—gardens in windy locations are less attractive to butterflies.
- Provide a shallow water source or puddling area. (See page 78.)
- Plant native shrubs and wildflowers that provide nectar that they sip with their straw-like proboscis. Plants with white or pale-colored flowers and strong musky scent, such as yucca and moonflower, will attract night-flying moths.
- Plant host plants for caterpillars.
- Never use pesticides in or near your butterfly garden.
- You can also add a butterfly feeder that holds rotting fruit. (See page 69.)

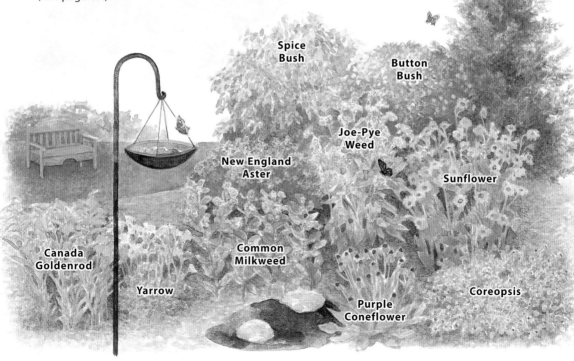

Examples here are for eastern U.S.

Amphibians and Reptiles

Providing places to raise young is important to wildlife beyond birds, bees, and butterflies. Reptiles and amphibians don't directly care for or raise their young, but they still need spaces to lay eggs or give birth and habitat where their young can survive.

Some snake species such as garter snakes give birth to live young, but most lay leathery-shelled eggs deposited in the ground or in a sheltered spot beneath rocks, woody debris, in mulch piles, or in dense vegetation, as do lizards and turtles. Amphibians such as frogs, toads, and many salamanders lay their eggs in jellylike masses or long strings in standing bodies of clean water. Some salamanders lay eggs in moist areas on land underneath rocks and woody debris. If they dry out, the embryos inside the eggs will die. Make sure your wildlife habitat garden has some

of these features so reptiles and amphibians can successfully reproduce. All of these places will also provide their young with safe hiding places where they can grow.

Water features designed for amphibian breeding should be well planted with native aquatic and wetland plants. These plants will provide cover for aquatic tadpoles and salamander larvae. Many amphibian species lay their eggs in temporary ponds called vernal pools that dry up in the summer or dry season. Because of this, vernal pools can't support fish, which are major predators of amphibian larvae. Without smaller, fishless ponds, many amphibians cannot survive in your yard or neighborhood. Keep this in mind when considering adding ornamental fish such as koi and goldfish, which will consume the eggs and young of aquatic amphibians.

A female skink guards her leathery-shelled eggs in a ground burrow.

Toads lay long strings of eggs in ponds and leave their young to care for themselves.

Nesting Places You Build

Wood ducks are one of dozens of cavity-nesting bird species that will lay eggs in nesting boxes installed in the landscape.

Restoring native plant communities and other natural landscape features will provide places to raise young for a diversity of native wildlife. You can also build or buy features to provide this important habitat component for specific groups of wildlife.

Nesting Boxes

Nesting boxes are often called "birdhouses" but birds don't actually live in them. They only use them for one purpose: as a place to raise their young. Nesting boxes mimic the natural cavities in trees that at least forty-six species of North American birds use for nesting. Bluebirds, chickadees, wrens, titmice, nuthatches, and woodpeckers are some of the species that commonly use nesting boxes, but so will certain species of swallows, warblers, flycatchers, ducks, and owls. While not cavity nesters, other species

HELP WITH NESTS

You can help birds find nesting material by building a brush pile, planting a meadow that offers plant stems, or placing pet hair, raw cotton, or natural fiber thread no more than 2 inches long (birds can get tangled in longer pieces of thread) outside in your wildlife habitat garden. Birds will gather these materials to build their nests.

Remember, insecticides not only negatively impact insect populations, they can affect birds' ability to capture enough food for their babies. Insects are the primary food source for baby birds. Without healthy insect populations, parent birds cannot feed their young. Many pesticides can harm or kill the birds themselves as well.

FAMILY PROJECT:
BUILD BIRD NESTING BOXES

Installing a nesting box is a fun project that will provide you with hours of wildlife viewing opportunities. Nesting boxes must be installed properly in order to provide a safe place for birds to bear and raise their young. Follow these tips to ensure birds successfully use your nesting boxes.

- Select a nesting box for functional purposes rather than decorative ones. Decorative boxes often lack the specific features that are attractive to birds.
- The entry hole must be the right size for the species you are trying to attract.
- The box dimensions and the distance from the entry hole to the floor of the box must be appropriate to accommodate different species' needs.
- The wood used should be at least ¾ inch thick to provide proper insulation.
- Natural, untreated wood is best. If you choose to stain or paint your nesting box, use a nontoxic product and only use it on the exterior.
- One side should open for monitoring and cleaning the box.
- The box should have ventilation holes drilled in the upper portion of the sides and drainage holes in the bottom.
- A sloping roof will allow water to run off and help keep the nest dry.
- Score the walls of the interior of the box to help baby birds leave the nest when they are ready to fledge.
- The box should not have a perch. Perches allow predators and non-native birds access to the nest. Special guards can be added to the entry hole and mounting pole to keep predators out.
- Cornell University's Lab of Ornithology is the recognized authority on nesting boxes for birds. Discover nesting box plans for dozens of species at *http://nestwatch.org/learn/all-about-birdhouses/*.

AMERICAN ROBIN AND BARN SWALLOW

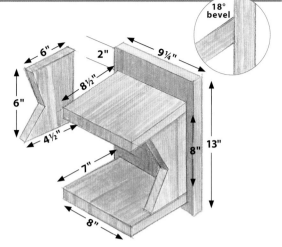

EASTERN/WESTERN BLUEBIRD

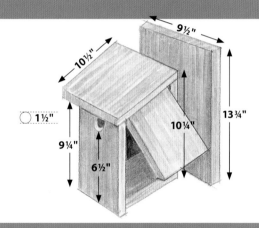

HOUSE WREN

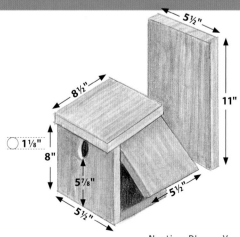

WILDLIFE PROFILE:
BLUEBIRDS

There are three species of bluebird in North America, the eastern, the western, and the mountain bluebirds, so no matter where you live you are likely to have a chance at spotting these azure-feathered beauties.

Not too long ago bluebirds were in trouble. By the middle of the last century their populations were rapidly declining due in large part to loss of nesting sites. Bluebirds are cavity nesters, and suburban sprawl and industrial agriculture were gobbling up land and removing the old trees and decaying rural fence posts used by bluebirds for nesting sites. The spread of aggressive non-native European starlings and house sparrows, which outcompeted native bluebirds for what nesting sites were left, pushed bluebirds into further decline.

Fortunately, in a perfect example of wildlife conservation on the neighborhood level, campaigns promoting the installation of special nesting boxes helped turn the tide for bluebirds, and their numbers have now stabilized.

To attract bluebirds, fill your yard with native plants. Bluebirds feed on berries and insects, so choose berrying trees and shrubs along with wildflowers native to your area. Native plants will feed bluebirds directly as well as through the insects they support. Don't spray pesticides. You can supplement natural foods with special bluebird feeders designed to offer dried mealworms. To offer nesting sites, try to keep dead or dying trees with cavities on your property, or install bluebird nesting boxes.

Avoid providing habitat for the invasive European starling (*Sturnus vulgaris*) and house sparrow (*Passer domesticus*).

including phoebes, mourning doves, robins, mallards, osprey, great horned owls, and even bald eagles will use nesting platforms.

Not all nesting cavities are created equal in the eyes of different bird species. Each species has specific requirements, ranging from hole size to depth of cavity. Your nesting box must meet these requirements for the species you wish to use it. Once your nesting box is discovered, your yard will become a flurry of activity as the birds begin nest building and feeding their young.

Monitoring your nesting boxes for invasive non-native species is important. Competition for nesting cavities with aggressive European starlings and English house sparrows was partially responsible for the decline of bluebirds, which have recovered in part because of people across the country installing and monitoring bluebird nesting boxes. Learn to identify these non-native species and their nests. If you discover starlings or house sparrows in your nesting boxes, you should remove their nests to discourage egg-laying.

Bat Houses

Bat houses provide these diverse and important flying mammals with a form of cover, but female bats will also use them as places to raise young. Species such as little brown bats and big brown bats will often gather in maternal colonies inside bat houses, where they give birth to and nurse their babies. The key to attracting a maternal colony of bats to a bat house is size. The bigger the better. Small bat houses won't support maternal colonies.

Bat houses are often used by female bat colonies as birthing places.

Young cottontails (above) are able to care for themselves as soon as they are able to leave the nest. Mother deer leave their fawns (right) hidden in the dense vegetation.

Finding Baby Animals

If you provide good places to raise young you'll be rewarded with baby animals in your wildlife habitat garden. Our protective instincts kick in at the sight of baby animals, and you might be tempted to "rescue" any babies you encounter. Resist that urge, because in most instances baby animals don't need rescuing and doing so usually reduces their chances of survival.

If you know for certain a baby animal has been orphaned or injured, the only appropriate thing to do is to contact a local wildlife rehabilitator. Wildlife rehabilitators have training and licensing to legally care for wildlife and return them to the wild. Do a web search or call a local nature center or county animal control agency to be put in contact with a rehabilitator.

Baby birds that are naked or covered in downy feathers are dependent on their parents for food and protection and should not be out of the nest.

Fledgling birds cannot fly when they leave the nest. It's normal for them to spend time on the ground and they don't need rescue.

Wildlife mothers are best at caring for their young. Often "rescuing" young animals is unnecessary and does more harm than good.

If you find a nestling on the ground, the best thing to do is to locate the nest and return the baby to it. The adult won't reject the baby because of human scent—in fact, most birds have poor sense of smell and won't even perceive human odor.

Once their flight feathers develop, young birds leap from the nest for their first flight and are then called fledglings. However, most birds don't master the ability to fly immediately. Some spend as long as two weeks in this fledgling stage. During this period, they hop around on the ground or in low vegetation exercising their wings and learning to fly. Their parents continue to feed and protect them throughout this fledgling period. If you find a fledgling, leave it alone. Many fledglings are picked up by well-meaning people who think they've been abandoned. While this is a vulnerable time for young birds it's a natural part of their life cycle.

The same is true for baby rabbits and deer. Rabbits give birth to their babies in shallow depressions in the vegetation lined with their fur, called forms. They only visit the babies twice a day to nurse them, which helps keep predators from finding the babies. Similarly, deer leave their newborn fawns hidden in the vegetation to protect them from predators. Unless you can confirm that the mother rabbit or deer has been killed, their babies don't need rescuing.

Squirrel mothers begin giving birth as early as late winter and can have several litters over the spring and summer. They give birth in a leafy nest built in the branches or inside tree cavities. If you find a baby squirrel on the ground with its eyes closed or that can't move, it's too young to be away from the mother and could be injured, dehydrated, or malnourished. Contact a wildlife rehabilitator immediately and do not try to feed or raise it yourself. Baby squirrels require special care and must be fed a specific formula every few hours around the clock.

Baby snakes, turtles, and lizards hatch from their eggs (or are born in the case of some snakes) completely equipped to care for themselves. Leave them right where they are. The best way to help them is to make sure you have plenty of native plants and other sources of cover, such as a brush or rock pile, in your yard to give them places to hide from predators.

If you unearth a nest of eggs in your yard (mulch and compost piles are favorite places for reptiles to lay eggs), leave them where they are or contact a wildlife rehabilitator for help relocating them. Embryos attach to the inside of the eggshell shortly after laying and moving the eggs could result in the death of the embryos if not done properly.

WILDLIFE PROFILE:
MONARCH BUTTERFLY

Monarch butterflies are one of the few insects that most people can identify. Their striking black and orange wings and black bodies with white polka dots make it easy (although viceroy butterflies, which co-mimic this coloration, are often mistakenly identified as monarchs). This familiarity is also due to the fact that monarchs can be found across most of the United States happily inhabiting backyards and gardens.

Female monarchs lay their eggs exclusively on milkweed, the monarch's only caterpillar host plant. The yellow and black-striped caterpillars feed on the milkweed leaves, absorbing the plant's toxins to make themselves distasteful to predators. The caterpillars grow and molt over the course of a couple of weeks, and then pupate and form a beautiful seafoam green chrysalis where they go through metamorphosis into their winged adult form. As adults, monarchs feed on flower nectar from a wide variety of native wildflowers, including milkweed.

One of the most striking things about monarchs is the fact that they are one of the few migratory insects. Two populations of monarchs exist in the North America, the eastern and the western, the latter found west of the Rocky Mountains. Each fall, the eastern population migrates south up to 3,000 miles to overwinter in the mountains outside of Mexico City. The western population migrates to central and southern California. In spring, they make the return journey, and over the course of four or five generations, repopulate the rest of the United States and lower Canada. The last generation hatched in late summer delays sexual maturity and undertakes the long-distance migration.

Sadly, populations of these iconic butterflies have plummeted in recent decades. Destruction of grassland habitats in their migratory corridors, logging around their wintering areas, overuse of pesticides, and the elimination of milkweed across rural, suburban, and urban areas are all contributing factors.

Planting a butterfly garden (see page 123) will not only help you attract monarchs to enjoy, it will actually help their populations recover. Simply plant clusters of native blooming wildflowers and don't spray pesticides. Be sure to include native milkweed so the female monarchs have a place to lay their eggs.

GARDEN FOR WILDLIFE™

NATIONAL WILDLIFE FEDERATION

You need to employ practices from **2+** of the following categories:

SOIL AND WATER CONSERVATION
☐ Limit Water Use
☐ Capture Rain Water from Roof
☐ Rain Garden
☐ Riparian Buffer (Plant Around Bodies of Water)
☐ Xeriscape (water-wise landscaping)
☐ Drip or Soaker Hose for Irrigation
☐ Use Mulch or Ground Cover to Retain Soil Moisture and Limit Erosion
☐ Reduce or Eliminate Lawn

CONTROLLING NON-NATIVE SPECIES
☐ Remove Non-native Plants and Animals
☐ Keep Cats Indoors
☐ Use Native Plants
☐ Reduce Lawn Areas

ORGANIC PRACTICES
☐ Eliminate Chemical Pesticides
☐ Eliminate Chemical Fertilizers
☐ Practice Integrated Pest Management
☐ Compost

CHAPTER SIX

Sustainable Garden Practices

Providing wildlife with the four components
of habitat outlined in earlier chapters—food,
water, cover, and places to raise young—will give
backyard wildlife a place to call home. How you
maintain that habitat is just as important. If you
create a wildlife habitat garden but continue to
spray pesticides, plant invasive non-native plants,
or waste water, you undo much of the benefit
to wildlife.

Sustainable gardening practices are the maintenance and management techniques you will use to keep your garden a healthy and attractive place for wildlife—as well as you and your family—while minimizing its potential negative effect on the greater ecosystem.

The Importance of Using Native Plants

Native plant and animal species are those that occur naturally in a given ecosystem and rely on each other for survival. When humans move a species from its native ecosystem to a new one, it is considered a non-native or "exotic" in the new area.

Don't confuse the introduction of a non-native species by humans with the natural dispersal of species. While species naturally expand their range into new ecosystems, this process typically takes hundreds of thousands of years. We are now artificially introducing species around the globe at a rate that is thousands of times faster than would occur naturally, and, unfortunately, non-native species can cause a host of problems to native species.

What Are Invasive Non-Native Species?

Some non-native species become invasive in their new ecosystems. They spread rampantly and compete with native species for space and resources because the predators or parasites that would naturally keep their population in check do not exist in the new area. Typically, invasive species are those that reproduce quickly and can survive in a variety of conditions. Left unchecked, invasive species can change diverse ecosystems into shadows of their former richness, pushing native species out and disrupting the natural balance. Native species cannot adapt to this abrupt introduction and spread of non-native species and as a result, natives decline, or in extreme cases actually go extinct, weakening the ecosystem.

Many of the worst invasive non-native plants were first introduced as garden plants. These plants were selected by the garden industry because they have ornamental qualities. While these plants might look nice in a garden, they do significant damage to local ecosystems when they "jump the garden fence" and spread into natural areas.

THE STORY OF PURPLE LOOSESTRIFE

One example of an invasive non-native garden plant is purple loosestrife (*Lythrum salicaria*), once a popular ornamental sold by nurseries across the country. It is native to Eurasia and grows in wet areas such as marshes, wet meadows, floodplains,

Ornamental purple loosestrife escaped the garden and invaded natural areas, degrading them. It is now banned in many places.

Japanese barberry is a bad invasive non-native plant that is still commonly sold.

Native birds, like this scarlet tanager, rely on native plants for survival.

and even roadside ditches. It has tall spikes of showy purple flowers that last all summer long. Its only problem is that it escaped human cultivation here in North America and took over natural wetland areas, pushing out native plant species and the wildlife that depends on them. In places where purple loosestrife has invaded, naturally diverse and productive wetland ecosystems that once supported hundreds of species of different native wetland plants, waterfowl, insects, amphibians, and their predators have now become barren monocultures. Fortunately, the dangers posed to natural areas by this invasive non-native plant have begun to be recognized, and it is now listed on many noxious weed lists and even banned in some states.

BE WARY OF COMMERCIAL ORNAMENTALS

Unfortunately, many other invasive plants are still commonly available for sale. One is Chinese wisteria (*Wisteria sinensis*). While this species of

Butterfly bush is a non-native that has escaped cultivation and has spread to wild areas where it destroys natural habitat. Plant native nectar plants for butterflies instead.

Chinese wisteria chokes out the native plant community (left). English ivy produces fruit when it grows up trees or buildings, allowing it to spread (right).

wisteria has beautiful lavender blossoms with an amazing scent, it can do serious ecological damage to native plant and wildlife communities. When it escapes and invades woodlands, it outcompetes or simply smothers dozens of species of woodland wildflowers, ferns, sedges, shrubs, and small trees, each with a unique collection of wildlife species that depend upon them. Japanese wisteria (*Wisteria floribunda*) is also invasive.

Just a few of the non-native ornamental garden plants that have proven to be invasive in different regions are burning bush (*Euonymus alatus*), Japanese barberry (*Berberis thunbergii*), saltcedar (*Tamarix* spp.), English ivy (*Hedera helix*), Norway maple (*Acer platanoides*), bamboo (*Phyllostachys* spp.), Japanese silvergrass (*Miscanthus sinensis*), Bradford pear (*Pyrus calleryana*), Chinese privet (*Ligustrum sinense*), periwinkle vinca (*Vinca minor*), South American pampas grass (*Cortaderia selloana*), Japanese honeysuckle (*Lonicera japonica*), Scotch broom (*Cytisus scoparius*), Canary Island date palm (*Phoenix canariensis*), and autumn olive (*Elaeagnus umbellata*). Sadly, the full list of invasive non-native ornamental plants would fill an entire book.

Even the beloved butterfly garden staple butterfly bush (*Buddliea* spp.) has escaped cultivation and is now a problematic invasive in the Pacific Northwest, the Mid-Atlantic and elsewhere. Choose native species instead.

Invasive Non-Natives vs. Aggressive Natives

The term "invasive" has a specific scientific meaning. Only non-native species that have been introduced either deliberately or accidentally by humans to a new ecosystem outside their native range and that spread rampantly to the detriment of native species can be called invasive. Ecologically, a native species cannot invade its own natural habitat and so cannot be called invasive.

This does not mean that some native plant species aren't aggressive and might not be the right fit for your garden space. In common gardening parlance such aggressive natives are sometimes called "invasive" but that's not the same thing as the ecological definition of an invasive species. If an aggressive native plant escapes the garden, it still provides the native wildlife with habitat and supports the ecosystem. Often, aggressive natives are pioneer species that are able to colonize disturbed areas and grow in poor soils. As they spread, their roots loosen the soil and their fallen leaves improve its nutrient levels. Other more particular native plants are then able to move in and eventually take over, and plant succession takes place. Invasive plants prevent other species from taking hold. When an invasive non-native plant escapes into the wild, however, it degrades the ecosystem by eliminating the native plants upon which wildlife rely. The difference is important to understand.

One example of an aggressive native is trumpet creeper (*Campsis radicans*). This woody vine is native to the eastern half of North America and is a popular garden plant. A natural "pioneer species" that evolved to rapidly colonize disturbed areas, such as when a tree falls in the forest letting more light in, trumpet creeper is

Native plants cannot invade their own natural habitat. Some, however, can be aggressive in gardens.

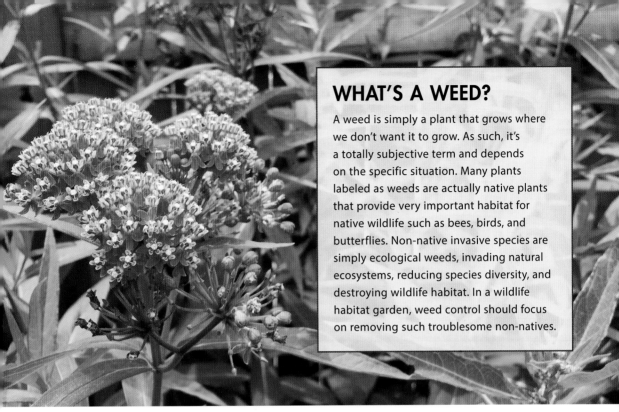

Many plants labeled as weeds are actually natives that provide habitat for wildlife such as bees, birds, and butterflies, such as this swamp milkweed (*Asclepias incarnata*).

an aggressive grower and can easily take over a small garden space if not kept in check. Unlike true invasive non-native species, however, if trumpet creeper "creeps" beyond the garden and into natural areas within its native range, it won't disturb the natural balance because it will simply play its natural role in the ecosystem, supporting wildlife by providing nectar to ruby-throated hummingbirds and long-tongued bees, and serving as the caterpillar host plant for the trumpet vine sphinx moth.

Non-Natives and Disease

In addition to the threat of becoming invasive, non-native plants can also harbor diseases that can kill native species. The American chestnut (*Castanea dentate*) was once the dominant tree in the eastern half of North America. In 1904,

an Asian chestnut disease was accidentally introduced to North America from exotic chestnuts planted in New York. American chestnuts had no natural defenses to this exotic blight, and it quickly became an epidemic. Today, there are no healthy mature American chestnuts left in North America.

Another example is the introduction of an exotic anthracnose (a type of fungus) in the 1970s that slowly kills the native Pacific dogwood (*Cornus nuttallii*) of the West and the flowering dogwood (*Cornus florida*) of the East. Pacific and flowering dogwoods coevolved with the wildlife species that share their native ranges, and they produce berries at the same time that birds begin their autumn migration.

Some evidence suggests that the exotic dogwood anthracnose was introduced by the Asian kousa dogwood (*Cornus kousa*), which is often used as

Flowering dogwood (top, left) and Pacific dogwood (top, right) produce small fruit timed to bird migration. Non-native kousa dogwood (bottom) produces large, hard-to-eat fruit out of sync with migration.

Bamboo forms dense stands where nothing else can grow.

Non-Natives and Wildlife

Another significant problem posed by the widespread use of non-native species is that they typically don't support any native wildlife. Most insects find them unpalatable, which is one reason they have been favored by the garden industry in the first place. As much as ninety percent of North American insects that rely on plants can only survive on the native plants with which they evolved. In areas dominated by invasive non-native plants, the local populations of insects can decline. Many wildlife species—birds in particular—depend on a steady source of insects to feed themselves and their young. Unfortunately, non-native plants continue to dominate the garden industry and as a result, our cities, towns, and neighborhoods, too. As we develop the land and replace native plants with non-natives, insect populations decline locally, and the birds and other wildlife that rely on them do, too.

Additionally, unlike native plants, non-native plants that don't become invasive typically require supplemental watering, fertilizer, and pesticide application to survive when used in landscapes and gardens. This maintenance costs you time and money. It can also cost wildlife. Because they need these additional supplements, non-native plants can contribute to pesticide and fertilizer pollution and the wasteful use of natural resources such as water.

an ornamental landscape tree. Kousa dogwood is much less susceptible to the anthracnose because it evolved with it, and can host it without fully succumbing to it, unlike native dogwoods. Because the anthracnose rarely kills kousa dogwood, landscape professionals often recommend planting it instead of Pacific or flowering dogwoods. While planting disease-resistant species makes sense from a conventional gardening perspective, it doesn't take into account the potential impact on wildlife. Kousa dogwood produces fruits that are twice as large as those of native dogwoods and are inedible to most birds. Unlike native dogwoods, it also produces those fruits out of sync with fall migration when the birds rely on the fruits to fuel their long journey. It might also be helping to spread the exotic anthracnose. Replacing native dogwoods with kousa dogwood is a bad ecological choice that could negatively affect migratory songbirds and other wildlife species that rely on those native species.

Replace Non-Native Plants

In any region, you'll find a great variety of native plant species that can meet your landscaping needs and are suited to almost every condition. Be sure to tell the local garden center or nursery that you'd like them to carry and label native plant species. In most cases, you can replace problematic non-native plants with native species that have similar ornamental or functional qualities in the landscape.

SERVICEBERRY FOR BRADFORD PEAR

Bradford pear (*Pyrus calleryana* 'Bradford') is a ubiquitously planted cultivar of a tree native to China. Despite the fact that it is a weak tree prone to storm damage, its beautiful white flowers in spring and compact branching structure have made this tree a favorite for landscapes across the country. Bradford pear, however, has little wildlife value other than to support European starlings. It has also begun to hybridize and escape cultivation, and is now considered an invasive plant in many areas.

A good native alternative to Bradford pear that will serve the same purpose in the landscape is serviceberry (*Amelanchier* spp.). Serviceberry is covered in beautiful white blossoms in the early spring and produces nutritious berries relished by many bird species, including waxwings, orioles, bluebirds, catbirds, and thrushes. In autumn, serviceberry leaves turn red, pink, or orange. Serviceberry is also commonly called juneberry or shadbush.

Collectively the following serviceberry species cover most of the United States and lower Canada:

- Allegheny serviceberry (*Amelanchier laevis*)
- Canadian serviceberry (*Amelanchier canadensis*)
- Downy serviceberry (*Amelanchier arborea*)
- Utah serviceberry (*Amelanchier utahensis*)
- Western serviceberry (*Amelanchier alnifolia*)

Replace this . . .

. . . with this

Follow Organic Practices

Synthetic chemicals manufactured by humans are some of our worst environmental pollutants, poisoning the air, water, and soil and killing wildlife. While many plants and animals naturally produce toxic chemicals, the volume and potency of those created by humans have made them a global conservation concern. Follow "organic" practices in your garden that don't rely on synthetic chemical pesticides and fertilizers.

Say No to Pesticides

Whether they target plants, insects, fungi, or mammals, pesticides are designed to kill. The best approach for a wildlife garden is to avoid their use altogether. Herbicides can kill off important native plants used by wildlife. Insecticides kill beneficial insects, such as pollinators and predatory insects,

Don't spray pesticides. There are many proven organic gardening techniques to control weeds that won't poison the local environment, such as burning them with a torch.

Pollinators such as butterflies (left) and bees (right) can be killed or weakened by plants treated with pesticides.

as well as pests. Rodenticides often kill predators from owls to bobcats to foxes that feed on poisoned rats and mice. Even pesticides derived from natural materials still kill wildlife.

Instead rely on organic gardening techniques such as:

- hand-picking pest insects from plants
- pulling weeds by hand regularly to prevent weeds from going to seed
- using a hand torch to burn weeds
- pouring boiling water or vinegar on weeds to kill them without using synthetic chemicals
- removing bird feeders if rats are feeding from them
- attracting beneficial insects and spiders to help control pests. Native ladybugs, mantids, lacewings, syrphid flies, tachinid wasps, and soldier beetles are just a few of the insects that prey on pests.

Brachonid wasps lay eggs on pest caterpillars. Rely on the natural pest control services of predators and parasites.

Fertilize without Fertilizer

Chemical fertilizers can make your lawn green, but they are also one of the biggest sources of water pollution. When it rains, fertilizers can be washed away into storm drains. This runoff ends up in local streams, rivers, and ultimately the ocean, where the excess nutrients disrupt the balance of those aquatic and marine ecosystems, killing wildlife or destroying its habitat.

Chemical fertilizers can also alter natural soil ecosystems, killing or repelling earthworms and other soil organisms that benefit plant roots.

Follow these tips to keep your plants healthy without using chemical fertilizers:

- Recycle yard "waste" like grass clippings, whole or shredded leaves, pine needles, chipped woody debris, or even old shredded newspaper by using it as mulch that will retain soil moisture, protect plant roots, and prevent erosion. Leave fallen leaves where they fall—this is nature's sustainable way of returning nutrients to the soil.

NEONICOTINOIDS

Neonicotinoids are a class of chemicals used as insecticides on crops and ornamental plants. They are currently the most widely used class of insecticides around the world. There are seven different neonicotinoid chemicals that can be found in hundreds of different products under various brand names.

Though they were developed in part out of concerns with toxicity of some earlier generation insecticides, there are increasing concerns with neonicotinoids themselves. That is because they are systemic, meaning that they are absorbed by all parts of the plant, including the sap and pollen, protecting it from chewing and sap-sucking insects. Once applied, they cannot be washed off.

Neonicotinoids not only affect targeted pest insects, but may also be harmful to nontarget beneficial pollinating insects including bees and butterflies, as well as moths, wasps, flies, and beetles. They may stay in soil for multiple years (and contaminate crops and other plants nearby, potentially causing impacts to pollinators), affect bees' ability to fly and feed, and interact with other pesticides to become more toxic. A large concern is the high occurrence of neonicotinoids in home garden products.

Determining if a plant has been treated with neonicotinoids is not always easy. There are no regulations requiring that plants treated with neonicotinoids be labeled. To guarantee you are purchasing plants that have not been treated with neonicotinoids, contact local plant nurseries—particularly those carrying native plants—and ask if their plants have been treated.

Cover crops such as clover can reduce the need for chemical herbicides and fertilizers.

- Plant cover crops such as buckwheat and clover between plantings in your vegetable garden or seasonal flower beds to enrich the soil. Turn cover crops into the soil before planting because as they decompose they add more nutrients to the soil.
- Create a compost pile, and add kitchen scraps (no meats, fats, or bones) along with layers of herbaceous plant debris. An equal amount of "browns" such as dead leaves and "greens" such as grass clippings will provide a balance of nutrients.
- Start vermicomposting, or composting with worms. You can purchase worms and put them in a plastic bin with moistened newspaper. Add fruit and vegetable scraps, eggshells, and other kitchen waste, and soon you'll have compost enriched with nutrient-rich worm castings.
- Urge your community to start a municipal leaf composting program. The community will gain access to free or inexpensive compost for enriching individual and community gardens.

You can enrich your soil by recycling kitchen and yard waste into compost. You can purchase or build a compost bin, create a wire compost cage, or simply create a pile.

COMPOSTING TIPS

- Add a handful of garden soil to inoculate your pile with microorganisms that break down materials and create compost.
- Do not let the pile dry out. Keep it evenly moist but not wet.
- Turn the pile with a pitchfork to aerate it. Turning also speeds up the composting process.
- Compost is ready to be used in the garden when it is black and crumbly.

"GREEN" MATERIAL

These materials add nitrogen to compost:

- Grass clippings
- Tea bags
- Coffee grounds and filters
- Seaweed (available in coastal areas)
- Eggshells
- Fruit and vegetable scraps
- Herbaceous garden clippings
- Manure from herbivores (cows, horses, goats, sheep, rabbits, guinea pigs, hamsters)

"BROWN" MATERIAL

These materials add carbon to compost:

- Dead leaves/needles
- Sawdust from untreated wood
- Wood ashes
- Black and white newspaper
- Wood shavings or small pet bedding

UNACCEPTABLE MATERIAL

These materials can produce odors, attract pests, or spread weeds or disease and should not be composted:

- Meat
- Bones
- Oils
- Dairy products
- Weed seed heads
- Dog, cat, or other carnivorous animal waste

COMPOST PILE CROSS SECTION

Coffee Grounds
Sawdust
Grass Clippings
Newspapers
Leaves

Conserve Water

Water is a precious resource and unfortunately a lot of it is wasted in our landscapes. Turf grass is the dominant landscape plant in America, and most species of turf grass are incredibly water-dependent. Lawns and other ornamental plants guzzle billions of gallons of water annually, water that could be going to agricultural fields, filling our reservoirs, and providing habitat for wildlife. What's worse, much of that water ends up evaporating in hot weather before it can even be utilized by lawns.

In urban and suburban environments, rainwater washes off impervious surfaces like roofs, driveways, sidewalks, and roads and flushes down storm drains rather than being absorbed to be used by plants and replenish the groundwater.

Follow these tips to conserve water in your wildlife habitat garden:

- Plant natives. Native plants are adapted to the natural rainfall levels of their native ecosystem so rarely need supplemental watering once established.

Collect rainwater in a rain barrel for use in the garden.

- Practice the art of xeriscaping, using drought-tolerant plants and landscape designs that don't require watering.
- If you must water, do it early in the morning before the heat of the sun can evaporate water away.
- Water using soaker hoses that deliver water directly to plant roots, rather than broadcasting water with overhead sprinklers.
- Mulch your beds, which helps the soil retain moisture for your plants.
- Collect rainwater for use in the garden in a rain barrel or cistern.
- Remove impervious surfaces and replace with garden beds or permeable pavers that allow water to percolate into the soil.
- Reduce the size of your lawn, or eliminate it altogether.

Native plants thrive under natural precipitation levels and usually don't require supplemental watering. If you must water, use drip irrigation or a soaker hose rather than a sprinkler. These methods apply water directly to the root zone of the plants, which reduces water loss due to evaporation.

Native plants (left) thrive in the local conditions and rarely need to be watered. Mulch (above) helps retain soil moisture.

Join the Movement

Creating a wildlife habitat garden with native plants seems like a simple thing, but it is actually a powerful action that you can take to save declining wildlife. It's the perfect way to "think globally, act locally."

You can join the National Wildlife Federation's growing network of other like-minded wildlife habitat gardeners by having your yard or garden recognized as a Certified Wildlife Habitat and getting involved beyond your backyard.

Wildlife habitat gardens are beautiful and diverse. Here, a squirrel tree frog rests on a cluster of beautyberries.

Certify Your Wildlife Habitat Garden

Your wildlife habitat garden can be recognized as a Certified Wildlife Habitat by the National Wildlife Federation. Certifying is as simple as following the guidelines in this book to provide the four habitat components—food, water, cover, and places to raise young—and practice sustainable gardening techniques such as eliminating pesticides, conserving water, and planting native species.

Aside from the rewards of offering wildlife a place to thrive, when you certify you get the following benefits:

- Inclusion in the National Wildlife Federation's national listing of Certified Wildlife Habitats
- A personalized certificate for your wildlife habitat
- A press release to share with your local media about your achievement
- A subscription to the National Wildlife Federation's *Garden for Wildlife* e-newsletter
- A free one-year membership to the National Wildlife Federation which includes a subscription to *National Wildlife®* magazine
- A 10% discount on nesting boxes, feeders, birdbaths, and other products from National Wildlife® catalog
- Eligibility to purchase and post an attractive Certified Wildlife Habitat yard sign to display your commitment to wildlife and the environment

Beyond these perks, by certifying your wildlife habitat garden you officially join the growing movement of people who are dedicated to the idea of "think globally, act locally" who have made a difference for local wildlife. By posting a Certified Wildlife Habitat yard sign, you help amplify the voice of the National Wildlife Federation in promoting wildlife habitat gardens as a personal conservation action to help wildlife. Certifying is a powerful act of grassroots activism that can inspire others to follow your lead. The biggest reward of all is getting to see the wildlife that benefit from your actions.

Posting a Certified Wildlife Habitat sign not only celebrates all you've done to help local birds, butterflies, and other wildlife, it helps spread the wildlife habitat gardening message to all of your neighbors.

Ready to Start?

Use our certification application checklist below to determine what habitat features you are already providing and get ideas for new features you'd like to add. When you check off the minimum number in each category, you are ready to certify! Just fill out our mobile-friendly online application at *www.nwf.org/garden*.

Food Sources

Plants provide the basic foods for wildlife. Feeders can be used as a supplemental source of food. Remember that some creatures will become food for others in a balanced habitat. Encourage a natural diversity of wildlife in your yard to ensure a healthy ecosystem. How do you provide food for wildlife? **(Minimum requirement: 3)**

NATURAL FOODS

☐ Seeds   ☐ Pollen

☐ Berries   ☐ Sap

☐ Fruits   ☐ Foliage/Twigs

☐ Nuts   ☐ Insects

☐ Nectar

SUPPLEMENTAL FEEDERS

☐ Seed Feeder

☐ Suet Feeder

☐ Squirrel Feeder

☐ Butterfly Feeder

☐ Nectar Feeder for Hummingbirds or Orioles

Water Sources

Wildlife needs a clean water source for drinking and bathing. How do you provide water for wildlife? **(Minimum requirement: 1)**

☐ Birdbath

☐ Shallow Dish

☐ Water Garden/Pond

☐ Butterfly Puddling Area

☐ Rain Garden

☐ Lake

☐ Stream/River

☐ Spring

☐ Seasonal Pool

☐ Ocean

Places for Cover

Wildlife needs shelter from bad weather and hiding places— for both predators and prey. How do you provide cover for wildlife? **(Minimum requirement: 2)**

☐ Wooded Area   ☐ Brush/Log Pile

☐ Dense Shrubs/Thicket   ☐ Rock Pile/Wall

☐ Bramble Patch   ☐ Burrow

☐ Meadow/Prairie   ☐ Cave

☐ Evergreens   ☐ Roosting Box

☐ Ground Cover   ☐ Water Garden/Pond

Places to Raise Young

In order to provide complete habitat, you must provide places for wildlife to engage in courtship behavior and to mate, and then to bear and raise their young. How do you provide places to raise young for wildlife? **(Minimum requirement: 2)**

☐ Mature Trees   ☐ Water Garden/Pond

☐ Dead Trees/Snags   ☐ Wetland

☐ Meadow/Prairie   ☐ Burrow

☐ Dense Shrubs/Thicket   ☐ Cave

☐ Nesting Box   ☐ Host Plants for Caterpillars

Sustainable Gardening Practices

You must maintain your garden in a natural, sustainable way. What sustainable gardening practices do you employ? **(Minimum requirement: 2 in at least 2 categories)**

SOIL AND WATER CONSERVATION

☐ Limit Water Use

☐ Capture Rainwater from Roof

☐ Rain Garden

☐ Riparian Buffer (Plant Around Bodies of Water)

☐ Xeriscape (water-wise landscaping)

☐ Drip or Soaker Hose for Irrigation

☐ Use Mulch or Ground Cover to Retain Soil Moisture and Limit Erosion

☐ Reduce or Eliminate Lawn

CONTROLLING NON-NATIVE SPECIES

☐ Remove Non-native Plant and Animals

☐ Keep Cats Indoors

☐ Use Native Plants

☐ Reduce Lawn Areas

ORGANIC PRACTICES

☐ Eliminate Chemical Pesticides

☐ Eliminate Chemical Fertilizers

☐ Practice Integrated Pest Management

☐ Compost

Already Certified?

You're eligible to post one of our yard signs to share your accomplishment. To log in and purchase a sign, head to *www.nwf.org/yardsign*.

Share Your Experience

As you develop your wildlife habitat garden, talk to your neighbors about your ideas, so they will understand the importance of restoring habitat and the landscape you are trying to create. Check with your local municipal authorities and homeowners' association regarding lawn care and weed control. In some areas, it may not be legal to establish a meadow or to create brush piles. Sometimes these regulations are based on safety principles like fire prevention, but often they are based on nothing more than conventional suburban landscaping aesthetics.

Since a naturalistic landscape can look very different from a conventional one, inform your neighbors of your plans. Try to educate them on the importance of restoring habitat and share with them the wonders of a sustainable wildlife habitat landscape whenever possible. Select native plant species that have ornamental value as well as habitat value. Add definition to your more wild-looking plantings with a mulched border or a mowed strip. Offer to share seeds or divisions of your native habitat-providing plants with neighbors. Hold an open house or neighborhood block party in your habitat to show neighbors the beauty of the habitat garden and to allow them to connect with wildlife. Join a garden club, or start one on your own, to teach others about the needs of wildlife and how gardens can be more than just pretty landscaping.

Remember, by creating a wildlife habitat garden, you become an ambassador for the idea of natural gardening. You can let your yard or garden grow completely wild, but if that look causes neighbors and local authorities to view wildlife gardens as a nuisance, you could be doing more harm than good. In those instances, you might go for a more ornamental look. If you're using native plants and maintaining your garden naturally, the wildlife will still benefit and your neighbors will be inspired to follow your example.

Beyond Your Backyard

By creating a wildlife habitat garden, you've demonstrated your commitment to making a difference for wildlife and the planet. Through the process, you've probably learned an incredible amount about how the actions you take in your own garden have an impact on the ecological health of your community. Take on new challenges and help spread the Garden for Wildlife message. Go beyond your backyard to help develop wildlife habitats throughout your community.

Schoolyard habitats. A wildlife garden at a school will not only help wildlife, it will offer endless outdoor education opportunities.

Workplace habitats. Many businesses have large properties that can be managed as productive habitat areas. By allowing these areas to "go natural," a significant amount of habitat can be restored.

Neighborhood open space. Homeowners' associations often oversee common grounds and other neighborhood open spaces that offer great opportunities for wildlife gardening and habitat restoration. Check with your local parks department about helping to make your town's park system an important resource for wildlife as well as people.

Faith habitats. The message of stewardship of the Earth is a key component of many religious traditions. What better way of expressing that sentiment than by giving some space back to our fellow creatures?

Habitats as places of healing. The opportunity to be surrounded by beautiful natural landscapes and to view wildlife can be therapeutic for all people. The staff and residents of hospitals, pediatric care units, long-term care facilities, and assisted living complexes can benefit from connecting with nature through a wildlife habitat garden.

Other Garden for Wildlife Initiatives

There are many ways you can get involved in creating wildlife habitat gardens and helping backyard wildlife beyond your own yard. The National Wildlife Federation has a host of programs and opportunities for you to get engaged in helping to create wildlife habitat gardens throughout your community.

SCHOOLYARD HABITATS

You can turn your schoolyard or other educational facility into a living outdoor classroom. Part of the Eco-Schools U.S.A. initiative, NWF's Schoolyard Habitats program provides interdisciplinary outdoor educational opportunities for students, educators, and community members. With nature and wildlife serving as both teachers and classroom, Schoolyard Habitats projects engage students in an active learning process that leads to improved achievement and heightened awareness about the natural world.

SACRED GROUNDS

The grounds of your church, synagogue, mosque or other place of worship can be turned into a habitat for local wildlife while helping you deepen your faith-based stewardship.

COMMUNITY WILDLIFE HABITAT

Entire communities have rallied together to restore wildlife habitat within their border. Each of these Community Wildlife Habitats have created hundreds or even thousands of individual Certified Wildlife Habitat gardens and held educational workshops, native plant sales and more to help community members create wildlife gardens.

MAYORS' MONARCH PLEDGE

Monarch butterfly populations have plummeted in recent years. In response, NWF launched the Mayors' Monarch Pledge to give guidance to and inspire community leaders to take actions to restore habitat for these iconic butterflies. Your community could be one of hundreds that have taken the pledge.

HABITAT STEWARDS

Become part of NWF's conservation army by going through our Habitat Stewards training and then helping others create wildlife habitat gardens throughout your community. Visit *www.nwf.org* to find out how to participate.

Glossary

***Bacillus thuringiensis* (Bt)** A type of soil bacteria used as an insecticide. Different strains of Bt are toxic only to specific groups of insect pests. Bt does not harm other forms of wildlife or humans.

Balled-and-burlapped A method of selling large woody plants where the root and soil ball is wrapped in burlap.

Bare-root A method of selling woody and herbaceous plants where the soil or other planting medium has been washed away from the root-ball.

Beneficial insect These are predatory insects that keep the populations of aphids, certain caterpillars, and other plant-eating garden pests in check.

Bog A type of wetland formed when dead vegetation accumulates in a body of water faster than it can decompose, forming peat.

Brush pile A pile of woody debris that is carefully constructed to provide cover and places to raise young for wildlife.

Bunch grass Grasses that form clumps and do not spread by vegetative runners as turf grass does. Most North American native grasses are bunch grasses.

Cavity nester A species that typically builds nests and bears its young in tree holes or other natural cavities.

Chloramine A chemical added to some municipal water sources that kills microorganisms. It is toxic to fish, amphibians, and aquatic invertebrates.

Communities The naturally balanced groupings of plants, wildlife, and other organisms in a self-supporting ecosystem.

Consumer Species that obtain nutrients by eating plants or other wildlife species. See Food chain.

Controlled burn A fire deliberately set and controlled to replicate the natural, periodic fires to which prairie and some forest plant communities are naturally adapted.

Conventional garden/landscape practice Gardening or landscaping practices that do not take the needs of wildlife into account. Conventional gardens and landscapes are made up primarily of lawn and ornamental plants.

Cultivar A specially bred or cloned variety of a plant.

Deciduous A plant that seasonally loses all of its foliage and goes dormant.

Decomposer An organism that obtains nutrients from the dead parts of plants or animals and returns nutrients to the soil. See Food chain.

Diatomaceous earth A nontoxic substance made up of tiny, sharp silica particles used to kill soft-bodied insect pests.

Ecology The branch of biology that studies the interactions among living organisms, as well as the interactions among living organisms and the surrounding environment.

Ecosystem Balanced, self-sustaining interactive communities of plants and wildlife.

Ectotherm A species that relies on environmental conditions to regulate body temperature rather than producing heat internally.

Edge effect The increase in the number of species that occurs where two ecosystems meet.

Emergent plant A plant species that naturally grows in wet soils and shallow standing water.

Evergreen A plant species that does not lose the majority of its foliage seasonally.

Exotic species See Non-native species.

Fallow field An agricultural field that is left unseeded and allowed to grow wild for a season or several seasons as a means of naturally restoring nutrients to the soil. Fallow fields are also used by wildlife.

Feral animal Domestic animal that is not cared for by humans. Feral animals prey on and compete with native species for resources.

Fledgling A young bird that has developed its flight feathers and left the nest but cannot fly. Fledglings spend several days on the ground or in low bushes and are fed by their parents.

Food chain The path of nutrients through the living components of an ecosystem. The food chain is made up of producers, consumers, and decomposers.

Forb An herbaceous plant that is not a grass.

Fungicide A pesticide designed to kill fungus.

Generalist species A species that can adapt to a variety of environmental conditions and can often live in close proximity to humans.

Girdling The process of killing woody vegetation by cutting through the outer bark around the entire base of the trunk and severing the plant's vascular system.

Gray water Water that is first used to wash clothing or dishes, and then it is used to water inedible landscape plants.

Green manure A crop turned into the soil rather than harvested. This is an organic method of returning nutrients such as nitrogen to the soil.

Habitat The collection of elements in an ecosystem that wildlife need to survive. The elements of habitat needed by all wildlife species are food, water, cover, and places to raise young.

Herbaceous plant A plant that has fleshy stems that die back to the ground during the dormant season.

Herbicide A pesticide designed to kill plants.

Herptile This is a collective term for reptiles and amphibians.

Host plant A plant that serves as a food source for butterfly and moth caterpillars.

Hybrid A type of plant created by crossing two varieties of plants.

Insecticide A pesticide designed to kill insects and other invertebrates.

Integrated pest management (IPM) An approach to pest control that strives to manage pests at acceptable levels rather than eliminating them completely. It begins with techniques that are least harmful to the environment, such as planting resistant varieties, using biological controls, and applying less toxic sprays, and only resorts to traditional synthetic pesticides when the other methods have failed.

Invasive species An exotic species that has been introduced by humans into a new ecosystem and that spreads rampantly, outcompeting and eliminating the species native to that ecosystem.

Marsh A treeless wetland area.

Meadow Transitional native grassland community that occurs in areas with enough rainfall to support the growth of trees.

Microclimate The climate of a small specific place within a larger area as contrasted with the climate of the entire area.

Monoculture An area where only one plant species grows. Commonly used in agricultural terms, but it also refers to areas infested by invasive exotic plants.

Mixed grass prairie Native grassland community that includes wildflowers and grasses that grow between 2 and 5 feet tall.

Mosquito dunk A product that contains a strain of the bacteria *Bacillus thuringiensis* that will kill mosquito larvae without affecting most other wildlife or humans.

Mulch Any material used to cover bare soil to prevent erosion, retain moisture, and protect plant roots. Materials used for mulch include chipped or shredded bark, dead leaves, grass

clippings, pine needles, straw, aged sawdust, shredded newspaper, gravel, and plastic.

Native species A species that evolved in an ecosystem over the course of thousands or millions of years and is part of that ecosystem's balanced community.

Naturalized species An exotic species that has established itself in the wild. Some naturalized species are invasive, while others are kept in check by the plants, animals, and other organisms native to the ecosystem.

Nestling A baby bird that has not developed its flight feathers and has not left the nest.

Non-native species A species introduced to a new ecosystem by human activity.

Organic Pest control and fertilization practices that are not chemically based.

Pesticide A substance used to eradicate a plant, animal, or other organism deemed to be a pest to humans.

Pioneer species Plant species that colonize disturbed areas and can thrive in poor soil conditions. Pioneer species improve soil conditions and allow other more particular plants to colonize.

Plug A young herbaceous or woody plant grown in a small container and sold with a small root-ball.

Pollination The process of moving pollen grains from the male parts of a flower to the female parts, resulting in fertilization and subsequent development of fruit and fertile seeds.

Pollinator A diverse group of wildlife that includes bees, butterflies, moths, flies, beetles, and other insects, as well as hummingbirds, bats, and other small mammals that are responsible for moving pollen and fertilizing plants.

Proboscis The straw-shaped mouthparts of butterflies and moths.

Producer Plants that use sunlight, water, and soil nutrients to create food for themselves in the form of carbohydrates. Producers are consumed by consumers. See Food chain.

Rain barrel A barrel attached to a drainage downspout that collects and stores rainwater to be used in the landscape.

Root zone The area in which the roots of a tree or other plant grow.

Savannah Grassland with scattered pockets of trees and shrubs.

Scavenger An organism that feeds primarily on carcasses of other animals that it has not killed itself.

Shortgrass prairie A native grassland community composed of wildflowers and grasses that grow less than 2 feet tall.

Snag A standing dead tree.

Specialist species A species that requires a unique set of conditions and environment in order to survive.

Succession The natural changes in plant communities that occur after a disturbance.

Suet Rendered animal fat that can be used as a high-energy food source for birds in winter.

Swamp A wetland that supports trees.

Tallgrass prairie Native grassland community composed of wildflowers and grasses that grow 5 feet or taller.

Turf grass Grass species that spread sideways by vegetative runners as well as by seed. Lawns are typically composed of turf grasses of European and Asian species.

Vermicomposting Process of composting where worms are used to consume waste materials and produce nutrient-rich castings.

Vernal pool A small temporary pond that fills and dries up seasonally. These pools do not support fish, making them excellent breeding places for amphibians.

Water garden A relatively small, human-made pond or other container that holds water and plants.

Weed A subjective term referring to any plant that is considered undesirable in a given location.

Weed ordinance A local law specifying landscape restrictions, such as the maximum allowable height of herbaceous vegetation or the presence of dead standing trees or brush piles.

Whip A branch cutting of a woody plant that can be planted directly into the ground where it develops a root system and forms a new plant.

Wildflower A generic term for flowering herbaceous plants that includes both native plants as well as naturalized and invasive ones.

Woody debris Fallen dead trees or parts of trees.

Woody plant Refers to plants that have rigid stems covered in bark that do not die back to the ground seasonally.

Index

Photo Credits

Cover photo (goldfinch) by Nathan Rees (age 13), *nathansnaturephotography.com*.

The following photographs were used with permission: **6** (middle) & **25** cedar waxwing, **36**, **74** (bottom) skunk courtesy of Leigh Scott Photography; **10**, **21**, back cover right courtesy of John C Magee; **27**, **33**, **150-151** courtesy of Scott Dressel-Martin/Denver Botanic Gardens; **69** courtesy of Anne Grimes; **82** top (moving falls) courtesy of Devin DePamphilis; **94** courtesy of North Creek Nurseries (*www.northcreeknurseries.com*); **106** top (chipmunk) courtesy of Kathy Harris; **114** top (doves) courtesy of Joni Mozis; **124** left (skink with eggs) courtesy of Kate Short; **91** top left (butterfly bush) courtesy of Cindy Golia

Many thanks to all the dedicated wildlife gardeners who donated their photos to the National Wildlife Federation. Your support allows us to reach more people with our wildlife conservation message: cover inset (monarch butterfly) Howard B. Cheek, **2** (Henslow's sparrow) Richard Remington, **6** bottom & **70** (hummingbird in water) Sandrine Bizlaux-Scherson, **8** Randy Streufert, **9** Don Gagnon, **22** Nancy Palmstrom, **23** Samira Blackwell, **24** Sam Wharton, **29** Connie Etter, **31** bottom left (phlox) Diann Stewart, **31** bottom right (sunflower) Daniel Noon, **38** Mavourneen Strozewski, **40** top (red eft) William Borne, **40** right (damselfly) John Bishop, **41** Debra Milne, **44** right (bee) Chuck Duplant, **45** top right (birch) Jillian String, **46** bottom left (lupine) Marian Herz, **46** bottom right (geranium) Jenni Lopez, **48** top (bee) J.R. Graham, **48** bottom (wasp) Mark Brinegar, **49** top (butterfly) Ron Wilson, **49** second from top (beetle) Carol Senske, **49** second from bottom (hummingbird) Charles Gonzalez, **49** bottom (bat) Don Bland, **51** Don Getty, **52** right (moth) Thomas McClanahan, **52** left (fritillary) Alfred Whiteley, **53** bottom right Patrick Carney, **54** Jenny Ragland, **55** top (pileated woodpecker) Edward Episcopo, **55** bottom

(finches) Mike Masterson, **56** Barbara Snyder, **59** Eldon Palmer, **60** Mary Braatz, **75** inset (tree frog) Wayne Morgan, **78** bottom (swallowtails) Andrea Popick, **79** Reg Daves, **83** Jack Kraft, **86** Karen Pierpont, **87** top (dragonfly) Alfonso Aguilar, **90** Jeanette Tasey, **93** middle left (holly) Michelle Miklik, **99** Diane Kinman, **102** Mary Brown, **107** right (roosting box) Jenni Lopez, **110** Jenni Lopez, **115** top (nesting owls) Rick Cuzner, **115** bottom (box) Jenni Lopez, **116** bottom (robins) Charles Huber, **122** Janie Walker, **128** top (Eastern bluebird) Jo Crebbin, **130** top (bunny) Patricia Bartie, **137** bottom right (scarlet tanager) Randy Streufert, **146** top left & back cover (butterfly) Kaye Franklin, **146** top right (bee) John Stahl, **146** (bottom) caterpillar Morgan Neff, **152** Julia Bartosh, **161** Debra Milne, **162** & back cover bottom (grey tree frog) Shanon Shuler-Gaskins, **163** Maralee Park, **164** Martha Hitchiner, back cover left top (bee) Brian Lensch, back cover left, second from top (gray fox) MJ Springett

Back cover author photograph courtesy of Noam Galai and BUILDseries

Photographs pages **61–68**, **121** by Amy Leinbach

Photograph page **129** courtesy of the National Wildlife Federation

Photographs pages **20**, **30**, **72**, **82** bottom, **98**, **124** right, **141**, **145** top, **155** courtesy of the author

Illustrations by Michele Farrar except page **127** (Northern Prairie Wildlife Research Center/North American Bluebird Society) and **108** (Bat Conservation International)

Getty: **11** bottom (wood thrush) Larry Keller, **92** top right (cedar) Philip Nealey, **114** bottom (Gila woodpecker) Genyphyr Novak, **109** bottom (insect hotel) Mint Images, **116** top (caterpillar) hopshomemade

Shutterstock: **5** ilikestudio, **7** top & **88** critterbiz, **7** middle & **112** Vitalart, **7** bottom & **134** Richard Pratt, **11** top Birdiegal, **12** romarti, **13** top left (notebook & pencil) Be Good, **13** top right (camera) Niphon Subsri, **13** bottom left (magnifying lens) Maria Isaeva, **13** bottom right (binoculars) Sebastian Enache, **14** emkaplin, **19** Ad_hominem, **28** JSvideos, **31** top right Diana Taliun, **31** top left watcher fox, **32** top rokopix, **32** bottom debra millet, **34** Christian Delbert, **35** A3pfamily, **39** top right kavcicm, **39** bottom right Jolanda Aalbers, **40** bottom left Martha Marks, **42** forestpath, **43** Paul Tessier, **44** left Steven R Smith, **45** bottom right Kathy Clark, **45** top left InspiringMoments, **45** bottom left Peter Turner Photography, **46** top left Bonita R. Cheshier, **46** top right Julian Popov, **47** top left Chris Alcock, **47** inset (hummingbird) Sari ONeal, **47** bottom right Sundry Photography, **47** top right T-I, **47** bottom left Prokuronov Andrey, **48** middle Jordan Roper, **50** Cathy Keifer, **53** top left Happy Dragon, **53** top right Leonid Eremeychuk, **53** bottom left photowind, **57** top left OnlyFOOD, **57** top center Abel Tumik, **57** top right Sarah Marchant, **57** middle left Yuriy Bartenev, **57** middle center FLariviere, **57** middle right FLariviere, **57** bottom left xpixel, **57** bottom center scherrsm, **57** bottom right Ozgur Coskun, **58** redtbird02, **74** top Al Mueller, **75** bottom Rostislav Stefanek, **78** left Gyuszko-Photo, **81** Angel DiBilio, **84** konzeptm, **85** Poh Smith, **87** bottom Manfred Ruckszio, **91** top right Jose Ignacio Soto, **91** bottom

left Kees Zwanenburg, **91** bottom right Przemyslaw Muszynski, **92** top left tanja-vashchuk, **92** center left Erika Kirkpatrick, **92** bottom left damann, **92** center right Nastyaofly, **92** bottom right Melinda Fawver, **93** top left Jerrold James Griffith, **93** bottom left steve estvanik, **93** top right Evannovostro, **93** center right Adam Gladstone, **93** bottom right Lynn Whitt, **95** top left hjochen, **95** bottom left valkoinen, **95** top right Kathryn Roach, **95** bottom right Green Dahlia, **96** top left Prokuronov Andrey, **96** bottom left Karel Bock, **96** top right Anna Gratys, **96** bottom right feawt, **97** top left Cozy Home, **97** bottom left Mikkey, **97** top right nnattalli, **97** bottom right tamu1500, **100** Christian Puntorno, **101** top Krazie Jedi, **101** bottom Hayley Crews, **103** FrankHastings, **105** bottom sirtravelalot, **106/107** bottom AZ Outdoor Photography, **109** top Zoroyan, **117** top DMS Foto, **117** bottom Tom Reichner, **118** Geoffrey Kuchera, **119** top Brian E Kushner, **119** bottom Jay Ondreicka, **120** Deatonphotos, **125** Feng Yu, **126** Peter K. Ziminski, **127** top left Tim Zurowski, **127** middle left Hayley Crews, **127** bottom left Steve Byland, **128** bottom left Eric Isselee, **128** bottom right Eric Isselee, **130** bottom Janet Griffin-Scott, **131** Bruce MacQueen, **132** William Saylor, **133** JHVEPhoto, **136/137** bottom Jay Ondreicka, **137** top Olga Koroleva, **138** bottom left Peter Turner Photography, **138/139** top fasthorses, **139** right Velimir Isaevich, **140** Agnes Kantaruk, **142** top left mustu7211, **142** top right Sundry Photography, **142** bottom Cameron Whitman, **143** blew_s, **144** top Darryl Brooks, **144** bottom mcajan, **145** bottom Floki, **147** ArTDi101, **149** Manuela Durson, **150** left DJTaylor, **151** right Maria Evseyeva